Light & Easy Diabetes Cuisine

Light & Easy

Diabetes

Cuisine

BETTY MARKS

SECOND EDITION

SURREY BOOKS
Chicago

....

Dedicated to those who work to find a cure for diabetes

LIGHT & EASY DIABETES CUISINE, 2nd Edition, is published by
Surrey Books, Inc., 230 E. Ohio St., Suite 120, Chicago, IL 60611.

Second edition: 2 3 4 5

This book is manufactured in the United States of America.

Library of Congress Cataloging-in-Publication Data

Marks, Betty
   Light & easy diabetes cuisine / Betty Marks,
      p. cm.
   Previously published: Los Angeles : HPBooks, 1990.
   Includes index.
   ISBN 1-57284-038-2 (pbk.)
   1. Diabetes–Diet therapy—Recipes. I. Title: Light and easy diabetes cuisine.
   II. Title.

RC662.M347 2001
641.5'6314–dc21

                                                            2001054210

For prices on quantity purchases or for a free book catalog, contact
Surrey Books at the above address.

Distributed to the trade by Publishers Group West

Cover photograph ©2001 Robert Olding. Courtesy of Photonica.

Acknowledgments

My special thanks go to the creative cooks who helped me with the testing and tasting of the recipes in this book. I am especially indebted to Rhonda Stieglitz for her recommendations and culinary ability. Nan Racusin and Nancy Henderson similarly offered their opinions, suggestions and cooking skills.

I am grateful to Hope Warshaw for her expert nutritional analyses that enhance each recipe and for her help in balancing them nutritionally and to Dr. Gerald Bernstein for his Foreword.

And not the least, to my many friends who listened to my concerns and were encouraging and supporting during the writing of this book.

About the Author

Betty Marks is a New York City literary agent by profession, but a cook for fun. She is the author of *The Diabetes Double-Quick Cookbook*, *The High Calcium, Low Calorie Cookbook*, and the originator and co-author of *The International Menu Diabetic Cookbook*. She has had insulin-dependent diabetes for 25 years, and it has not stopped her from enjoying ballroom dancing, swimming, hiking, and photography.

Contents

Preface

··

In spite of the constraints that diabetes puts on life, it is well worth the challenge of cooking carefully and eating well to maintain the best possible health. My life is busy and filled with many different activities and pleasures, leaving limited time to prepare complex meals. Because I have discovered an efficient system of organization and meal planning, I am able to create appealing and tasteful meals for myself, friends, and family. These meals can be prepared quickly and easily and will meet the nutrition and exchange requirements for those whose diabetes is controlled by diet, pills, or insulin. You can have a delicious and interesting meal on the table in under an hour.

The recipes in *Light & Easy Diabetes Cuisine* include suggestions for appetizers, soups, entrees, grains, pasta, vegetables, salads, baked goods, dressings, sauces, and desserts—more than enough choices for appealing and balanced meals. Although some of the recipes may be new to you, the ingredients can be found in your local supermarket, and I've specified fresh ingredients wherever possible.

Hope S. Warshaw, M.M.Sc., R.D., C.D.E., nationally known diabetes educator and author, has calculated the nutritional breakdown of the recipes based on the American Diabetes Association and American Dietetic Association exchange lists. Preparation times precede each recipe, but may vary according to the cook's expertise and the size of the cooking equipment used.

What is required to prepare a variety of nutritious and tasty meals is organization, planning, and efficient techniques. Here are some time-saving tips to make your meal preparation truly *Light & Easy:*

- stock your larder with the basic staple items frequently called for in these recipes

- before you prepare a recipe, read it through carefully, and assemble all the ingredients and tools you will need on your counter, in order of use
- make stocks, dressings, and marinades in advance and store in the fridge or freezer
- keep your measuring cups and spoons where you can easily find them. Diabetes control means portion control
- a blender, steamer basket, and food processor speed along food preparation
- a large chef's knife makes chopping easier
- cleaning up as you go means less cleanup later

I hope you will enjoy preparing and eating these many dishes and that you have much time left to enjoy life's other bounties!

Betty Marks
New York, New York

A Note From a Nutritionist

Eating well, living fast, and controlling diabetes might sound like an incompatible trio. Today, in our fast-paced world, healthy eating practices are often left in the dust when numerous other responsibilities and activities take priority. And that prioritizing may compromise your general good health and diabetes management. Unfortunately, many people believe that preparing meals with fresh, wholesome ingredients requires hours and hours. Thus, cooking becomes a task reserved for special occasions. Frozen, convenience, and fast foods often become the quick and easy fare to eat day in and day out. In *Light & Easy Diabetes Cuisine*, Betty Marks demonstrates that meal preparation can be quick and healthful for people with or without diabetes and, most important, pleasing to the palate.

As a dietitian and diabetes educator, the most common complaint I hear is that the diabetes meal plan lacks interest. The lists of allowed foods appear limited, and the methods of preparing these foods result in tasteless, unimaginative meals. Just glancing at some of the recipes in *Light & Easy Diabetes Cuisine* disproves this notion. Betty Marks incorporates many unique ingredients and utilizes a wide variety of quick cooking methods to provide new ideas for creative meal planning, often the most difficult part of diabetes management.

At present the goals for diabetes meal planning are quite similar to the goals being touted for all Americans. Keep the fat content down, especially saturated fat. Increase the amount of starches, grains, fruits, and vegetables you eat, and eat less protein. The guidelines are reflected in these recipes.

Each recipe provides the food exchange calculations for one serving. The food exchange values put forth by the American Diabetes Association and American Dietetic

Association were utilized. Each recipe has been evaluated for calories, carbohydrate, protein, total fat and sodium content. As there is a great emphasis on lowering cholesterol and saturated fat in the diet, each recipe is also analyzed for its content of cholesterol, saturated fat, polyunsaturated fat, and monounsaturated fat. When observing these figures, think about keeping cholesterol down to less than 300 milligrams per day. Your total calories from fat intake should be 30% of total calories, or less, with 10% or less being contributed by saturated fat. Polyunsaturated fat should contribute about 10%, and the remaining 10% should come from monounsaturated fats such as olive oil.

The majority of the nutrient and exchange information provided for these recipes was calculated with the computer program *Recipe Analysis and Exchange List Conversion* developed by Lawrence Wheeler, M.D., Ph.D., and Madelyn Wheeler, M.S., R.D., C.D.E. The nutrient values in the program were obtained from a variety of resources but mainly the United States Department of Agriculture's *Handbooks for Composition of Foods*, 1976-1988. In addition, the current United States Department of Agriculture's *Handbooks for Composition of Foods* were used in conjunction with the second edition of *The Nutrition Almanac* from Nutrition Search, Inc., and several other references.

After perusing *Light & Easy Diabetes Cuisine*, and adding a few new recipes to your repertoire, you'll likely agree that eating well, living fast, and managing diabetes are a compatible trio.

Hope S. Warshaw. M.M.Sc., R.D., C.D.E.
Nutrition Consultant
Alexandria, Virginia

Hints for Planning & Preparation

Meals should be planned to provide a balance chosen from the essential food groups, with your individual exchange plan in mind. Milk, grains, fruit, vegetables, meat and fat all contribute to your good health. Know the number of calories you need for each meal during the day for your daily grand total. The calorie counts and nutritional breakdown at the end of each recipe will give you instant access to the information you need. Adding the numbers will help you decide which selections to include in your daily meal plan. Vary your food choices so that there are good balances of whole grains and seeds, fish, milk and fresh vegetables.

HOW-TO HINTS

Blanching: Vegetables retain their nutrients and crispness if plunged into boiling water about 2 minutes and then refreshed quickly under cold water.

Making Bread Crumbs: Place toasted or day-old whole-wheat bread in a food processor and process to make fine crumbs. Store in a tightly closed container and keep in the freezer.

Beating Egg Whites: Let egg whites stand at room temperature before beating with the electric mixer. A little cream of tartar may be added to stabilize the beaten whites.

Freezing: Freeze summer berries such as strawberries, raspberries, blueberries and vegetables such as bell peppers. Herbs such as chives, basil, parsley, oregano and dill may be frozen for use throughout the year.
Berries: Hull strawberries and pick over blueberries, blackberries and raspberries, discarding any bad ones. Do not wash but spread them on a baking sheet and place in freezer until solid. Transfer to plastic freezer bags or plastic containers, label and store in freezer until ready to use.

Defrost before using unless making a yogurt "ice cream" in which case they go straight into the blender.
Peppers and herbs: Trim, chop and freeze on baking sheets; pack as for berries.

Julienne: To make julienne strips of bell peppers, citrus zest, carrots, celery, endive, zucchini or other vegetables, trim away curved or damaged parts and cut into matchstick-shaped slices about 2 inches long and 1/4 inch wide.

Preparing Lobster: Fill a large kettle with 1 inch of water and bring to a boil. Place live lobster head first into pot and cover. Steam about 7 minutes until lobster turns red. When cooked, remove from pot and lightly push shells away from body to drain out excess fluid. Crack claws with a nutcracker. Use a sharp knife to split lengthwise and remove the hard sand sac located between the eyes. All other parts of the lobster may be eaten.

Preparing Nuts: *Blanching:* Drop nuts such as almonds or hazelnuts into boiling water 2 minutes. Drain nuts and rub off skins. Nuts may then be chopped or used whole.
Roasting: Spread in a baking pan, sprinkle with a little cinnamon and bake in preheated 350F (175C) oven about 15 minutes. Store in a tightly closed container.

Toasting Seeds: Heat a non-stick skillet and add sesame, sunflower or pumpkin seeds. Cover and warm seeds until they begin to pop. Shake pan to keep from burning. Remove and spread on paper towels to absorb any released oils. Store in a covered jar in refrigerator.

Soup Stocks: Make large batches of vegetable or chicken broth on your day off. Skim off any fat that accumulates (this is readily done if you place the broth in the refrigerator for a few hours until fat hardens on surface). Store in small containers in the freezer and defrost ahead of time for use in recipes. To make small quantities, pour into ice cube trays, then remove and store in plastic freezer bags. To make vegetable stock, see recipe page 9.

Crushing Garlic: Crush large cloves of garlic with the side of a large knife; they may then be easily peeled and minced. It is possible to purchase chopped garlic in jars, with a preservative; however the flavor is not as profound.

Chopping Onions: Slice off ends, peel and, with a large sharp knife, cut down to base of onion. Then turn and cut across to make squares. Then place onion on side and slice through to get rough chopped pieces.

Peeling Vegetables: Use one of the vegetable peelers available in cookware departments for a fast job of peeling carrots, turnips, potatoes, apples and other fruits and vegetables.

Organizing: Before starting to prepare the recipe, read it over carefully to make certain all ingredients are on hand. Arrange ingredients on the counter in order of their use. Do all the chopping and cutting before starting, unless there is waiting time in which to do so. The piles of chopped vegetables may then be picked up and utilized as needed.

ABBREVIATION GUIDE

Chol: Cholesterol
Carbo: Carbohydrate
Prot: Protein

Fat*
Sat: Saturated
Poly: Polyunsaturated
Mono: Monounsaturated

The calories in each food are determined by the amount of fat (9 calories per gram) and carbohydrate and protein (4 calories per gram) it contains.

Cholesterol is found only in animal products, such as meat, butter or cheese, not in plant products.

* Fats are either saturated, polyunsaturated or monounsaturated depending on their chemical composition. Saturated fats are usually solid at room temperature, for example, butter or lard. Corn oil, soybean oil and safflower oil are examples of polyunsaturated fats. Peanut oil, olive oil and canola oil are monounsaturated fats.

Basics

Certain basic recipes are referred to in the ingredients lists of many recipes. Chicken Broth (page 12) and Betty's Butter (page 11) are frequently called for and can be made ahead and stored in the freezer. These two essentials form the foundation of many good soups, meat, poultry or grain dishes.

The Graham Cracker Crust and the Perfect Pie Crust can be used for chilled fruit pies or filled with some of the creamy concoctions included here and in the Dessert chapter. The pie crust recipe can be used to make individual tarts.

The mayonnaise and cream cheese recipes can be used with main courses, salads, appetizers, even dessert. After tasting these basics, the adventurous cook will find that they serve many purposes.

Please note that frozen apple juice concentrate can be substituted in equal amounts for fructose in any of the recipes.

VEGETABLE STOCK

There are two equally good methods for preparing a rich vegetable base for soup or sauce. The first is simply collecting the water left from cooking various vegetables. Blend together and store in refrigerator up to two days.

The second method uses a collection of the scrubbed vegetable parings and unused tops and excess vegetable pieces. Collect them in a plastic bag and refrigerate. Every day or two place in a saucepan, add water or vegetable juices, bring to a boil and simmer about 30 minutes. Strain, place in small containers (or in an ice cube tray) and freeze until ready to use.

Count as no calories or exchanges since amounts are negligible.

Basic White Sauce

Serves: 4 (1/4-cup) servings
Cooking time: 5 minutes
Preparation time: 5 minutes

1 tablespoon Betty's Butter (page 11)
1 tablespoon arrowroot
1 cup evaporated skim milk
1/8 teaspoon salt
1/8 teaspoon white pepper

Heat butter in a small non-stick skillet, then stir in arrowroot. Gradually add milk; cook, stirring, until sauce thickens. Stir in salt and pepper.

Per Serving:
108 Calories, 5mg Chol, 9g Carbo, 5g Prot, 137mg Sodium, 3g Fat (0.9g Sat 1.1g Poly 0.8g Mono)

Exchanges: 1 milk, 1/2 fat

Variations: For thicker sauce add more butter and more arrowroot for each cup of milk.
Cheese Sauce: Add 1/4 cup shredded low-fat cheese to hot sauce; cook, stirring, until melted.
Per Serving:
108 Calories, 11mg Chol, 10g Carbo, 7g Prot, 291mg Sodium, 5g Fat (2.1g Sat 1.1g Poly 0.8g Mono)

Exchanges: 1 milk, 1/2 fat

Betty's Butter

Serves: 32 (1-tablespoon) servings
Cooking time: 0
Preparation time: 5 minutes

1 cup whipped butter, softened
1 cup polyunsaturated oil, such as safflower,
sunflower seed, corn, vegetable, walnut or a
combination

Place ingredients in a blender or a food processor fitted with
the metal blade. Process until mixed. Place in a plastic container; store in freezer. Makes 2 cups.

Per Serving:
34 Calories, 4mg Chol, 0g Carbo, 0g Prot, 14 mg Sodium, 4g Fat
(1.2g Sat 1.5g Poly 1.0g Mono)

Exchanges: 1 fat

Variations: *Herb Butter:* Blend with dill, mustard, garlic, gingerroot,
tarragon, chives or other herbs.
For a small amount, just combine 1 tablespoon oil with 1 tablespoon
butter and melt in a saucepan.

Chicken Broth

Serves: 6 (1-cup) servings
Cooking time: 1 to 2 hours
Preparation time: 20 minutes

1 broiler-fryer chicken, skin removed
4 garlic cloves
2 celery stalks with tops, coarsely chopped
6 parsley sprigs
1 bay leaf
6 peppercorns
2 medium-size onions, cut in quarters
1 carrot, sliced
1 parsnip, sliced
8 cups water

In a large kettle, bring all ingredients to a boil. Cook, uncovered, over low heat 15 minutes; skim off any froth that accumulates. Reduce heat, cover and simmer 1 to 2 hours. Remove cover and let cool. Strain, pressing meat to draw out liquid. Save chicken pieces for use in salads or other dishes. Discard other solids. Refrigerate. Skim off any hardened fat. Broth must be used within 3 days or frozen for future use. Makes 6 cups.

Per Serving:
20 Calories, 2mg Chol, 3g Carbo, 2g Prot, 15 mg Sodium, 0g Fat
Exchanges: free

Cottage Cream Cheese

Serves: 16 (1-tablespoon) servings
Cooking time: 0
Preparation time: 5 minutes

1 tablespoon non-fat milk powder
2 tablespoons unsalted whipped butter
2 tablespoons walnut oil
1 cup low-fat (1%) cottage cheese

In a blender or a food processor fitted with the metal blade, mix all ingredients together. Refrigerate, covered. Makes about 1 cup.

Per Serving:
37 Calories, 4mg Chol, 1g Carbo, 2g Prot, 60mg Sodium, 3g Fat (1.0g Sat 1.1g Poly 0.8g Mono)
Exchanges: 1 fat

Variation: Season with herbs, chives, green onions, or as desired.

Ricotta Cream Cheese

Serves: 16 (1-tablespoon) servings
Cooking time: 0
Preparation time: 5 minutes

1/3 cup part-skim ricotta cheese
3/4 cup low-fat (1%) cottage cheese

In a blender or a food processor fitted with the metal blade, process cheeses until smooth. Makes 1 cup.

Per Serving:
14 Calories, 2mg Chol, 1g Carbo, 2g Prot, 60mg Sodium, 1g Fat (0.3g Sat 0g Poly 0.1g Mono)

Exchanges: free

Variation: To make a fruit topping, add 2 teaspoons of sugar-free fruit conserve, such as raspberry, apricot or peach, for each cup of cheese.

Yogurt Sour Cream

Serves: 16 (1-tablespoon) servings
Cooking time: 0
Preparation time: 5 minutes plus few hours drip time

16 ounces plain low-fat yogurt or non-fat yogurt

Place yogurt in a cheesecloth- or coffee filter-lined sieve and let drip over a bowl in the refrigerator 4 to 6 hours, or overnight, until the yogurt has the consistency of thick sour cream. Reserve whey for other uses. Makes 1 cup.

The whey that drips out can be reserved for use in making soups, breads or cooked vegetables.

Per Serving:
22 Calories, 1mg Chol, 3g Carbo, 2g Prot, 0mg Sodium, 0g Fat
Exchanges: free

Variations: *Flavored Yogurt Sour Cream:* For a sweet flavor, add cinnamon, vanilla extract or thawed frozen orange juice concentrate. For savory dishes, add herbs, such as dill, tarragon, parsley or caraway, to yogurt before placing in sieve.

Make-Believe Mayo

Serves: 16 (1-tablespoon) servings
Cooking time: 0
Preparation time: 5 minutes

1 cup low-fat (1%) cottage cheese
2 tablespoons safflower oil
1 tablespoon apple cider vinegar
1/4 teaspoon salt
Dash white pepper

In a blender or a food processor fitted with the metal blade, process all ingredients until smooth. Refrigerate, covered, at least 24 hours before using. Makes 1 cup.

Per Serving:
27 Calories, 1mg Chol, 1g Carbo, 2g Prot, 76mg Sodium, 2g Fat (0.4g Sat 1.1g Poly 0.5g Mono)

Exchanges: 1/2 fat

Variation: Combine with tomato paste, mustard, pickles or herbs, as desired.

Graham-Cracker Crust

May be used with cream cheese or fruit fillings, topped with yogurt, or used with one of the suggested fillings from the dessert section.

Serves: 8 servings
Cooking time: 10 minutes
Preparation time: 10 minutes

14 graham-cracker squares (1 cup crumbs)
2 tablespoons walnut oil

Preheat oven to 350F (175C). Place crackers in a blender or a food processor fitted with the metal blade. Process crackers to crumbs. Add walnut oil to the crumbs in blender or processor and combine. Pat down firmly in an 8-inch pie pan. Bake 10 minutes. Remove and let cool before filling. Makes 1 (8-inch) crust.

Per Serving:
60 Calories, 0mg Chol, 5g Carbo, 1g Prot, 47 mg Sodium, 4g Fat (0.6g Sat 2.4g Poly 1.2g Mono)
Exchanges: 1/2 starch/bread, 1/2 fat

Perfect Pie Crust

Fill with fruit or one of the cream cheese or thick yogurt mixtures.

Serves: 8 servings
Cooking time: 10 minutes
Preparation time: 30 minutes

1/2 cup whole-wheat flour
1/2 cup unbleached all-purpose flour
1/4 teaspoon salt
3 tablespoons safflower oil
About 3 tablespoons iced water
2 tablespoons buttermilk
Egg white

Preheat oven to 350F (175C). In a medium-size bowl, sift flours and salt together; stir in oil, 3 tablespoons water and buttermilk, adding more water if necessary. Knead dough three or four times, until moist and elastic. Shape into a ball, cover, and refrigerate 15 minutes. Place between two sheets of waxed paper and roll dough into a 12-inch circle. Place in an 8-inch pie pan. Trim edges and finish by pressing with a fork, or flute. Brush with egg white and refrigerate 10 minutes. If baking the shell empty, prick with a fork and weight with dry beans. Bake 10 minutes or until golden-brown. To make tart shells, use a cup to cut the dough and bake in muffin cups. Makes 1 (8-inch) crust.

Per Serving:
109 Calories, 0mg Chol, 12g Carbo, 2g Prot, 66mg Sodium, 6g Fat (0.8g Sat 3.4g Poly 1.4g Mono)
Exchanges: 1 starch/bread, 1 fat

Appetizers

Some people like to start their dinner with a small appetizer to take the edge off their hunger, or to have something to munch while the dinner is being prepared. Here are some appetizers that can be easily prepared and eaten with crackers, tortilla chips, pita triangles, celery, carrots or other fresh vegetables. The inventive chef can also create some original concoctions using low-fat (1%) cottage cheese, yogurt or part-skim ricotta cheese mixed with beans, artichoke hearts, caraway seeds, curry, salmon, pimento, dill, onion, shrimp, olives or almost anything that strikes his or her fancy.

Avocado Dip

Serve dip with toasted corn tortilla chips, Crudités (page 28) or whole-wheat crackers.

Serves: 20 (1-tablespoon) servings
Cooking time: 0
Preparation time: 15 minutes

1 medium-size ripe avocado, peeled
2 garlic cloves, chopped
Juice of 1-1/2 limes
1/4 teaspoon salt
1/4 cup plain low-fat yogurt
Pepper to taste
Few dashes red (cayenne) pepper

Cut avocado into chunks. In a blender or a food processor fitted with the metal blade, process avocado, garlic and lime juice to a puree. Add remaining ingredients and process until smooth.

Per Serving:
21 Calories, 0mg Chol, 1g Carbo, 0g Prot, 25mg Sodium, 2g Fat (0.3g Sat 0.2g Poly 1.1g Mono)

Exchanges: 1 tablespoon—free, 2 tablespoons—1 fat

Variation: *Guacamole:* Add 1 teaspoon chili powder and 1 small tomato, chopped.

Black Bean & Salmon Appetizer

This may be served on a bed of lettuce as a first course for four people.

Serves: 19 (2-tablespoon) servings
Cooking time: 0
Preparation time: 20 minutes

8 corn tortillas
1 (16-oz.) can black beans, rinsed and drained
1 (7-oz.) can pink salmon with bones, drained
2 tablespoons safflower oil
1/4 cup fresh lime juice
1/4 cup chopped fresh parsley
1/2 teaspoon onion powder
1/2 teaspoon celery salt
3/4 teaspoon ground cumin
3/4 teaspoon minced garlic
1/2 teaspoon grated lime zest
1/4 teaspoon dried red pepper flakes
1/4 teaspoon chili pepper

Preheat oven to 350F (175C). Cut tortillas in triangles and toast in oven until crisp, about 5 minutes. Combine the beans and salmon, flaking the salmon with a fork. Mix in remaining ingredients; chill to blend flavors. Serve with tortilla chips.

Per Serving:
68 Calories, 3mg Chol, 8g Carbo, 4g Prot, 75mg Sodium, 2g Fat (0.3g Sat 1.1g Poly 0.5g Mono)
Exchanges: 1/2 low-fat meat, 1/2 starch/bread

Caviar Cheese Dip

Serve with whole-wheat crackers, or Crudités (page 28). This is also delicious as a topping for baked potatoes.

Serves: 16 (1-tablespoon) servings
Cooking time: 0
Preparation time: 5 minutes

3/4 cup part-skim ricotta cheese
1/4 cup low-fat (1%) cottage cheese
1 teaspoon fresh lemon juice
2 ounces red lumpfish caviar

In a medium-size bowl, blend the cheeses together with lemon juice. Place in a serving dish and top with caviar, or stir in caviar, if desired.

Per Serving:
52 Calories, 54mg Chol, 2g Carbo, 5g Prot, 169mg Sodium, 3g Fat (1.3g Sat 0.6g Poly 0.8g Mono)
Exchanges: 1 meat

Lemon Tofu Dip

Serve as a dip for fresh vegetables or as a dressing for artichokes, fish or grains.

Serves: 32 (1-tablespoon) servings
Cooking time: 0
Preparation time: 10 minutes

1 lemon, cut into pieces
2 dashes sesame oil
1 cup soft tofu (bean curd)
1/2 cup buttermilk
1/2 teaspoon prepared horseradish
1 teaspoon Dijon-style mustard
1/4 teaspoon salt
Pepper to taste
1 tablespoon ripe olives, chopped (optional)

Place lemon pieces in a blender or a food processor fitted with the metal blade; add oil and process until lemon is cut into small pieces. Add remaining ingredients and process until smooth. Refrigerate until chilled. Makes 2 cups.

Per Serving:
7 Calories, 0mg Chol, 1g Carbo, 1g Prot, 2 mg Sodium, 0g Fat
Exchanges: free

Salmon Dill Dip

Serve with rice crackers, whole-wheat crackers or vegetable crudités.

Serves: 12 (2-tablespoon) servings
Cooking time: 0
Preparation time: 10 minutes

1 cup low-fat (1%) cottage cheese
5 ounces canned pink salmon with bones, drained
1 tablespoon minced green onion
1 teaspoon fresh lemon juice
2 tablespoons chopped dill pickles
Dash hot-pepper sauce
Salt and pepper to taste

In a blender or a food processor fitted with the metal blade, process cottage cheese and salmon until blended. Stir in remaining ingredients to combine. Makes about 1-1/2 cups.

Per Serving:
31 Calories, 6mg Chol, 1g Carbo, 5g Prot, 167mg Sodium, 1g Fat (0.4g Sat 0.3g Poly 0.3g Mono)
Exchanges: 1/2 low-fat meat

Spinach Dip

Serve with fresh garden vegetables, such as red or green pepper strips, celery, carrots or broccoli.

Serves: 16 (2-tablespoon) servings
Cooking time: 0
Preparation time: 15 minutes

8 ounces fresh spinach
8 ounces tofu (bean curd), cut in chunks
3 tablespoons fresh lime juice
1 tablespoon safflower oil
2 garlic cloves, minced
1 teaspoon dried leaf oregano, crushed
Dash nutmeg
Pepper to taste

Wash spinach leaves and spin or pat dry. Trim off tough stems. In a blender or a food processor fitted with the metal blade, place spinach and remaining ingredients and process until blended. Refrigerate to blend flavors. Makes about 2 cups.

Per Serving:
23 Calories, 0mg Chol, 1g Carbo, 2g Prot, 12mg Sodium, 2g Fat (0.2g Sat 0.1g Poly 0.4g Mono)
Exchanges: free

Caviar Endive Appetizer

Serves: 6
Cooking time: 0
Preparation time: 10 minutes

Yogurt Cheese, see below
2 heads Belgian endive
1 tablespoon grated lemon zest
1 ounce red or black lumpfish caviar

Yogurt Cheese:
12 ounces plain low-fat yogurt

Prepare Yogurt Cheese. Cut off ends of endive and separate leaves. In a small bowl, combine lemon zest with Yogurt Cheese and spoon a teaspoon of mixture onto each leaf. Top with caviar and arrange in a circle on a serving plate. Makes about 20 appetizers.

Yogurt Cheese:
Place yogurt in a cheesecloth- or coffee filter-lined sieve. Drain over a bowl in the refrigerator for a few hours until it has the consistency of cream cheese. Reserve whey for other uses. Makes about 6 ounces of cheese.

Per Serving:
38 Calories, 33mg Chol, 4g Carbo, 4g Prot, 128mg Sodium, 1g Fat (0.3g Sat 0.4g Poly 0.3g Mono)
Exchanges: 1/2 meat

Clam-Stuffed Celery

Serves: Makes 12 stuffed celery stalks
Cooking time: 0
Preparation time: 15 minutes

1 (10-oz.) can minced clams, drained, liquid reserved
1/2 cup part-skim ricotta cheese
1 garlic clove, minced
1 tablespoon fresh lemon juice
1 teaspoon minced onion
1/8 teaspoon red (cayenne) pepper
3 tablespoons snipped dill, or 1 teaspoon dried dill
  weed
6 celery stalks, cut in half crosswise

Place all ingredients except dill and celery in a blender or a food processor fitted with the metal blade and process until smooth. Add clam liquid if needed to thin; stir in the dill. Stuff celery stalks with cheese mixture. Makes about 1-1/4 cups filling.

Per Serving:
63 Calories, 23mg Chol, 2g Carbo, 7g Prot, 78mg Sodium, 3g Fat
(1.5g Sat 0.4g Poly 0.4g Mono)
Exchanges: 1 meat

Crudités

Any number of other fresh vegetables can be used instead of or in addition to those listed, such as broccoli, cauliflower, tender asparagus, snow peas, zucchini or summer squash.

Serves: 6
Cooking time: 0
Preparation time: 15 minutes

1 red bell pepper, julienned
1 green bell pepper, julienned
8 green onions
2 medium-size carrots, cut in half, julienned
8 radishes, trimmed
8 cherry tomatoes
2 celery stalks, halved lengthwise and crosswise

Arrange vegetables on a serving platter or in a basket. Serve with any of the sauces recommended for dipping.

Per Serving:
26 Calories, 0mg Chol, 6g Carbo, 1g Prot, 21mg Sodium, 0g Fat
Exchanges: 1 vegetable

Hot Cucumber Cups

Unpeeled zucchini or yellow squash may be used instead of cucumbers.

Serves: 6 to 8
Cooking time: 0
Preparation time: 15 minutes

2 medium-size cucumbers
1/4 cup part-skim ricotta cheese
1/4 cup low-fat (1%) cottage cheese
2 tablespoons chopped green onion
1 garlic clove, minced
1 tablespoon minced canned jalapeño chile
1 tablespoon chopped fresh parsley

Peel cucumbers and cut crosswise in 1-inch pieces. Scoop out most of seeds with a small spoon or melon baller, and drain on paper towels. Blend cheeses, green onion, garlic, chile and parsley; spoon into the cucumber cups. Makes about 16 hors d'oeuvres.

Per Serving:
10 Calories, 1mg Chol, 1g Carbo, 1g Prot, 24mg Sodium, 0g Fat
Exchanges: free

Bean Curd Spread

Serve on warm pita bread triangles topped with alfalfa sprouts, or serve with fresh garden vegetables. Miso is available in health food stores or Chinese markets.

Serves: 16 (2-tablespoon) servings
Cooking time: 0
Preparation time: 10 minutes

1 cup tofu (bean curd), cut into chunks
3 tablespoons miso (see Note at left)
1/4 cup water
1 teaspoon sesame oil
1 tablespoon fresh lemon juice
1/4 teaspoon hot red chili powder
2 green onions, chopped
2 tablespoons crunchy peanut butter
3 tablespoons plain low-fat yogurt

Place ingredients in a blender or a food processor fitted with the metal blade; process until smooth. Makes 2 cups.

Per Serving:
24 Calories, 0mg Chol, 1g Carbo, 2g Prot, 70mg Sodium, 2g Fat (0.3g Sat 0.7g Poly 0.7g Mono)

Exchanges: 2 tablespoons—free, 4 tablespoons—1/2 meat

Tuna Stuffed Mushrooms

Serves: 12
Cooking time: 0
Preparation time: 15 minutes

1 (3-1/4-oz.) can water-packed tuna, drained
1/4 teaspoon dried dill weed
2 teaspoons Dijon-style mustard
1 tablespoon fresh lime juice
12 capers, drained and chopped
12 medium-size mushrooms, stems removed
Parsley sprigs
Paprika

Mash tuna together with the dill, mustard, lime juice and capers in a small bowl. Stuff mushrooms with tuna mixture; garnish with parsley and a dash of paprika.

Per Serving:
21 Calories, 11mg Chol, 1g Carbo, 2g Prot, 51mg Sodium, 1g Fat
(0.1g Sat 0.4g Poly 0.3g Mono)

Exchanges: 1 mushroom cap—free; 3 mushroom caps—1 low-fat
meat, 1/2 vegetable

Stuffed Mushrooms

Serves: 6 (2-mushroom) servings
Cooking time: 0
Preparation time: 20 minutes

6 ounces part-skim ricotta cheese
1 teaspoon Dijon-style mustard
1 garlic clove, minced
12 large mushrooms, stems removed
Lemon juice
1 tablespoon chopped parsley
Dash paprika

Mix cheese with mustard and garlic in a medium-size bowl. Dip mushrooms in lemon juice. Stuff mushrooms with cheese mixture; sprinkle with parsley and a dash of paprika.

Per Serving:
48 Calories, 8mg Chol, 4g Carbo, 4g Prot, 47mg Sodium, 2g Fat (1.3g Sat 0.1g Poly 0.6g Mono)
Exchanges: 1 vegetable, 1/2 fat

Soups

Soup is a wonderful way to start a meal. There are hundreds of variations, from simple broths to complex vegetable combinations. A good, hearty soup may make the entire meal when served with a good bread or muffin, and a salad. Most of the soups included in this chapter use vegetables as the base thereby providing minerals and fiber.

Low-fat buttermilk, skim milk, non-fat yogurt and non-fat dry milk form the base for my "cream" soups. The Vichyssoise in this chapter is a sane and healthful variation of a rich classic French potage. Yogurt should not be boiled, but rather added to a soup, off the heat, to finish it.

Vegetable or chicken broth form the base of many soups. In a pinch, however, the addition of a little low-sodium chicken or vegetable bouillon granules will add the needed flavor.

When using a blender or a food processor to puree soup, never pour hot liquid directly into the container. Let it cool a little and add in small increments, then return to the saucepan to reheat.

Broccoli Soup

Serve cold with a sprinkling of sesame seeds.

Serves: 4 (1-1/4-cup) servings
Cooking time: 10 minutes
Preparation time: 10 minutes

1 teaspoon olive oil
1 small onion, chopped
1 garlic clove, minced
3 cups broccoli flowerets and stems
2 cups buttermilk
1 teaspoon cumin seed
1 tablespoon toasted sesame seeds

In a large non-stick skillet, heat oil. Add and sauté onion and garlic. Add broccoli and stir-fry 3 minutes until bright green. Place with remaining ingredients except sesame seeds in a blender or a food processor fitted with the metal blade. Process in batches until smooth.

Per Serving:
119 Calories, 5mg Chol, 15g Carbo, 9g Prot, 102 mg Sodium, 4g Fat (1.0g Sat 0.7g Poly 1.6g Mono)
Exchanges: 1/2 milk, 1 vegetable, 1 fat

Chickpea Soup

Serves: 6 (1-cup) servings
Cooking time: 25 minutes
Preparation time: 10 minutes

1 teaspoon virgin olive oil
1 small onion, chopped
1 garlic clove, minced
1 celery stalk, sliced
1 carrot, sliced
1/2 small red bell pepper, diced
1 cup canned Italian plum tomatoes with liquid
1/2 teaspoon dried leaf basil, or 1-1/2 teaspoons
   chopped fresh basil
1 cup canned chickpeas (garbanzos), rinsed, drained
4 cups Chicken Broth (page 12)
Pepper to taste

In a non-stick saucepan, heat the oil and cook onion, garlic and celery 5 minutes. Add remaining ingredients. Bring to a boil, reduce heat and simmer, covered, 20 minutes.

Per Serving:
74 Calories, 0mg Chol, 13g Carbo, 5g Prot, 96mg Sodium, 1g Fat (0.2g Sat 0.2g Poly 0.5g Mono)
Exchanges: 1 starch/bread

Cream of Mushroom Soup

Serves: 4 (1-cup) servings
Cooking time: 15 minutes
Preparation time: 10 minutes

1 teaspoon olive oil
2 shallots, chopped
1 celery stalk, sliced
12 mushrooms, sliced
2 cups skim milk
1-1/2 tablespoons whole-wheat flour
1/4 teaspoon salt
Pepper to taste
Dash ground nutmeg
2 tablespoons dry sherry
Paprika
1 tablespoon chopped fresh parsley

In a non-stick saucepan, heat oil. Sauté shallots and celery until softened; add mushrooms and cook until tender, about 5 minutes. In a blender or a food processor fitted with the metal blade, place remaining ingredients except paprika and parsley and process until combined. Add the mushroom mixture and process until pureed. Pour into saucepan and heat gently, stirring until soup thickens. Garnish with a dash of paprika and parsley.

Per Serving:
82 Calories, 2mg Chol, 11g Carbo, 5g Prot, 183mg Sodium, 2g Fat (0.3g Sat 0.2g Poly 0.9g Mono)
Exchanges: 1/2 milk, 1 vegetable

Cucumber Buttermilk Soup

Serves: 4 (1-1/4-cup) servings
Cooking time: 0
Preparation time: 10 minutes

2 cups peeled, seeded, chopped cucmbers
4 cups buttermilk
1 tablespoon fresh lemon juice
2 tablespoons chopped green onion
1 tablespoon chopped fresh mint, or 1 teaspoon drled
  leaf mint
1 tablespoon fresh dill, or 1 teaspoon dried dill weed
1 teaspoon ground cumin
Dash white pepper
1 tablespoon chopped fresh parsley

Place all ingredients except parsley in a blender or a food processor fitted with the metal blade and process until smooth. Garnish with parsley. Serve cold.

Per Serving:
108 Calories, 9mg Chol, 14g Carbo, 9g Prot, 259mg Sodium, 2g Fat (1.4g Sat 0.1g Poly 0.6g Mono)
Exchanges: 1 milk, 1/2 vegetable

Golden Carrot Soup

This soup can be served hot or cold.

Serves: 4 (1-1/4-cup) servings
Cooking time: 30 minutes
Preparation time: 10 minutes

1 tablespoon olive oil
1 pound carrots, sliced
2 cups Vegetable Stock (page 9)
1/4 teaspoon dried leaf thyme
1 bay leaf
1 teaspoon frozen orange juice concentrate
Pepper to taste
1/2 teaspoon grated gingerroot (optional)
1 cup skim milk
1 tablespoon chopped fresh parsley

In a non-stick medium-size saucepan, heat oil; add carrots and cook, stirring, about 10 minutes. Add stock and bring to a boil. Reduce heat and add thyme, bay leaf, orange juice and pepper; add gingerroot, if desired. Simmer until carrots are tender, about 8 minutes. Skim off any froth that accumulates; remove bay leaf. In a blender or a food processor fitted with the metal blade, process soup in batches. Return to saucepan; add enough milk for desired consistency. Heat, stirring. Garnish with parsley. Makes 5 cups.

Per Serving:
92 Calories, 1mg Chol, 13g Carbo, 3g Prot, 75mg Sodium, 4g Fat
(0.6g Sat 0.3g Poly 2.5g Mono)
Exchanges: 2 vegetable, 1 fat

Dilled Cauliflower Soup

This soup can be served hot or cold.

Serves: 4 (1-1/4-cup) servings
Cooking time: 25 minutes
Preparation time: 10 minutes

4 cups Vegetable Stock (page 9)
8 ounces cauliflower
1 leek
2 tablespoons chopped dill, or 2 teaspoons dried dill weed

Heat stock in a saucepan. Trim leaves and tough stems from cauliflower and break into flowerets. Wash leek well, trim and cut off most of green leaves. Coarsely chop leek. Add vegetables to stock and bring to a boil. Cover, reduce heat and simmer 20 minutes. In a blender or a food processor fitted with the metal blade, process soup in batches to a puree. Return to saucepan, stir in dill and reheat, if necessary.

Per Serving:
50 Calories, 0mg Chol, 9g Carbo, 3g Prot, 24mg Sodium, 0g Fat (0.1g Sat 0.2g Poly 0g Mono)
Exchanges: 2 vegetable

Fresh Vegetable Soup

Other vegetables can be added or substituted, such as zucchini, squash, parsnips, bok choy, cabbage, etc.

Serves: 4 (1-1/4-cup)
Cooking time: 25 minutes
Preparation time: 10 minutes

4 cups Chicken Broth (page 12)
2 turnips, diced
2 celery stalks, sliced
1 medium-size onion, chopped
2 parsley sprigs
2 carrots, sliced
1 bay leaf
1/2 teaspoon dried leaf oregano
Pepper to taste

Place all ingredients in a large saucepan. Bring to a boil. Cover, reduce heat and simmer 20 minutes until vegetables are tender. Skim off any froth that accumulates. Remove bay leaf before serving.

Per Serving:
44 Calories, 0mg Chol, 8g Carbo, 1g Prot, 53mg Sodium, 0g Fat
Exchanges: 1-1/2 vegetable

Mexican Corn Chowder

Serves: 6 (1-cup) servings
Cooking time: 25 minutes
Preparation time: 10 minutes

1 teaspoon corn oil
1 cup chopped onion
1 garlic clove, minced
1/4 cup chopped hot yellow chile
1/2 cup chopped green bell pepper
1 cup diced tomatillos (Mexican green tomatoes) or
    regular green tomatoes
2 cups fresh whole-kernel corn, or 2 cups canned or
    thawed frozen corn
2 cups Vegetable Stock (page 9)
Salt and pepper to taste
2 cups skim milk
1/4 cup diced red bell pepper

In a non-stick saucepan, heat oil; add onion and garlic; cook until softened. Add chile, green bell pepper, tomatillos, corn and vegetable stock. Cook 10 to 15 minutes. Season with salt and pepper. Remove about 1 to 1-1/2 cups of the soup and cool slightly. Place in a blender or a food processor fitted with the metal blade and process until pureed. Return to saucepan containing vegetables and add milk. Heat just to a simmer. Serve in warm soup bowls and garnish with diced bell pepper.

Per Serving:
100 Calories, 1mg Chol, 20g Carbo, 5g Prot, 84mg Sodium, 1g Fat (0.2g Sat 0.6g Poly 0.3g Mono)
Exchanges: 1 vegetable, 1 starch/bread

Oriental Snow Pea Soup

Serves: 4 (1-1/4-cup) servings
Cooking time: 12 minutes
Preparation time: 15 minutes

4 cups Chicken Broth (page 12)
2 large mushrooms, sliced
1 garlic clove, minced
1 teaspoon grated gingerroot
1 teaspoon low-sodium soy sauce
5 ounces tofu (bean curd)
1 cup snow peas, trimmed
1/4 cup minced green onions

In a saucepan, place Chicken Broth, mushrooms, garlic, gingerroot and soy sauce; bring to a boil. Cover, reduce heat and simmer 5 to 7 minutes. Cut tofu into 1/2-inch cubes. Add tofu and snow peas to broth; cook 2 minutes more. Garnish with green onions.

Per Serving:
69 Calories, 2mg Chol, 7g Carbo, 7g Prot, 20mg Sodium, 2g Fat (0.3g Sat 1.0g Poly 0.4g Mono)
Exchanges: 1/2 low-fat meat, 1 vegetable

Split Pea Soup

....

Serves: 4 (1-cup)
Cooking time: 45 minutes
Preparation time: 10 minutes

1 cup green or yellow split peas
6 cups water
1 tablespoon low-sodium chicken or vegetable
 bouillon granules
1 carrot, sliced
1 onion, quartered
Pinch dried leaf marjoram
Pinch dried leaf thyme
Dash red (cayenne) pepper
1 teaspoon imitation bacon bits

Rinse split peas; soak overnight if possible. In a large saucepan, place all ingredients except bacon bits. Bring to a boil.
Cover, reduce heat and simmer 45 minutes until tender. If a
smooth soup is desired, process in a blender or a food processor fitted with the metal blade. Return to saucepan to warm
before serving; add bacon bits for a meaty taste.

....

Per Serving:
184 Calories, 0mg Chol, 33g Carbo, 13g Prot, 28mg Sodium, 1g Fat
(0.1g Sat 0.3g Poly 0.1g Mono)
Exchanges: 2 starch/bread, 1 meat

Stracciatella Soup

Serves: 4 (1-cup) servings
Cooking time: 15 minutes
Preparation time: 5 minutes

1 egg plus 1 egg white
1-1/2 tablespoons semolina flour or whole-wheat flour
2 tablespoons grated Parmesan cheese
4 cups Chicken Broth (page 12)
1 tablespoon chopped fresh parsley

In a small bowl, mix eggs, flour, cheese and 1/4 cup of the cold broth until smooth. Meanwhile, bring remaining broth to a boil in a medium-size saucepan. Slowly add egg and flour mixture to broth, stirring gently. Cook, stirring, about 10 minutes. Garnish with chopped parsley.

Per Serving:
65 Calories, 73mg Chol, 5g Carbo, 6g Prot, 101mg Sodium, 2g Fat (.9g Sat .2g Poly .8g Mono)

Exchanges: 1 low-fat meat

Summer Soup

Serves: 4 (1-cup) servings
Cooking time: 25 minutes
Preparation time: 20 minutes

2 cups water
Salt and pepper to taste
2 new potatoes, peeled, diced
2 carrots, sliced
6 fresh spinach leaves, chopped
1/2 cup fresh green peas or thawed frozen green peas
1 tablespoon arrowroot
1-1/2 cups skim milk
1/4 teaspoon red (cayenne) pepper
1 tablespoon chopped fresh parsley

In a medium-size saucepan, place water, salt, pepper, potatoes and carrots; bring to a boil. Cover and cook 10 minutes. Add the remaining vegetables and cook 5 minutes more. Meanwhile, make a paste of the arrowroot and 3 tablespoons of the milk. Add remaining milk and stir into the vegetables. Add cayenne and simmer 5 minutes, until vegetables are tender. Garnish with parsley.

Per Serving:
97 Calories, 2mg Chol, 18g Carbo, 6g Prot, 112mg Sodium, 0g Fat
Exchanges: 1/2 milk, 2 vegetable

Tomato Soup

Serves: 4 (1-cup) servings
Cooking time: 10 minutes
Preparation time: 10 minutes

1/2 teaspoon vegetable oil
1 garlic clove, minced
1 shallot, minced
1 teaspoon arrowroot
1 (16-oz.) can Italian plum tomatoes
1 bay leaf
2 cups skim milk, room temperature
1/2 teaspoon dried leaf tarragon
1/8 teaspoon pepper

In a non-stick saucepan, heat oil; brown garlic and shallot. Add arrowroot and stir to blend. Meanwhile, in a blender or a food processor fitted with the metal blade, process tomatoes until pureed. Add tomatoes and bay leaf to saucepan and bring to a boil. Reduce heat, add milk, tarragon and pepper and heat slowly. Remove bay leaf, and serve.

Per Serving:
78 Calories, 8mg Chol, 12g Carbo, 5g Prot, 259 Sodium, 1g Fat (0.3g Sat 0.5g Poly 0.3g Mono)
Exchanges: 1/2 milk, 1 vegetable

Vichyssoise

Serves: 4 (1-cup) servings
Cooking time: 15 minutes
Preparation time: 15 minutes

1 cup Chicken Broth (page 12)
1 medium-size potato, peeled, diced
2 leeks, well washed, sliced
2 cups skim milk
1/4 teaspoon salt
Pepper to taste
1 tablespoon part-skim ricotta cheese
1 tablespoon chopped chives

In a blender or a food processor fitted with the metal blade, process broth, potato and leeks until smooth. Pour into a saucepan and cook until potato is tender, about 15 minutes. Place remaining ingredients, except chives, in blender or food processor with cooked vegetable mixture, and process again until smooth. Chill before serving. Garnish with chives.

Per Serving:
73 Calories, 3mg Chol, 12g Carbo, 5g Prot, 146mg Sodium, 1g Fat (0.3g Sat 0.1g Poly 0.1g Mono)
Exchanges: 1 skim milk

Variation: Add some tomato juice, chopped cucumbers or even a little chopped sweet potato.

Zucchini Soup

Serves: 6 (1-cup) servings
Cooking time: 15 minutes
Preparation time: 15 minutes

2 cups Chicken Broth (page 12)
2-1/2 cups sliced zucchini
1 cup chopped onion
2 garlic cloves, minced
Pinch dried leaf marjoram
1 teaspoon curry powder
Salt and pepper to taste
2 tablespoons non-fat dry milk
1 cup plain low-fat yogurt
1 teaspoon fresh lemon juice
2 tablespoons diced red bell pepper, or pimento

In a medium-size saucepan, place all ingredients except yogurt, lemon juice and bell pepper; bring to a boil. Reduce heat, skim off any froth that accumulates, cover and simmer 10 minutes or until zucchini is tender. Cool. In a blender or a food processor fitted with the metal blade, process in batches until pureed. Add yogurt and lemon juice; chill well. Garnish with bell peppers.

Per Serving:
39 Calories, 3mg Chol, 7g Carbo, 3g Prot, 75mg Sodium, 0g Fat
Exchanges: 1/2 milk, 1 vegetable

Poultry

Chicken and turkey are good entree choices since they are easy to prepare, can be cooked in a variety of ways, are low in fat and cholesterol, and they combine well with vegetables and sauces. Poaching skinned boneless chicken or turkey cutlets provides easily cooked morsels for use in salads, curries or chicken a la king.

Removing the skin from chicken before using will eliminate excess fat. It is actually easier to skin the whole bird than the parts. To remove the skin from a chicken: point the legs toward you and using a paper towel to grasp the skin, pull back the skin from the neck toward you, continuing to pull over entire chicken and cutting skin as necessary.

Keep poultry refrigerated until ready to cook. Wash all implements and surfaces that have come in contact with uncooked poultry with soap and water to avoid possible salmonella infection. Use a plastic cutting board rather than a wooden one. Rinse chicken with cold water before cooking.

The poultry recipes included here use a variety of methods, but all are easy to cook.

Argentine Corn Chicken

Serve this dish with Bell Pepper Salad (page 182).

Serves: 4
Cooking time: 40 to 45 minutes
Preparation time: 10 minutes

1 broiler-fryer chicken (about 2-1/2 lbs.), cut up
Salt to taste
Pepper to taste
1 tablespoon virgin olive oil
1 onion, sliced
2 garlic cloves, minced
2 tomatoes, diced
1 bay leaf
1/4 teaspoon dried leaf marjoram
1 cup frozen whole-kernel corn, thawed

Remove skin from chicken. Season with salt and pepper. In a large non-stick skillet, heat oil and cook chicken until tender, turning, 15 to 20 minutes. Remove from skillet and keep warm. Sauté onion and garlic in skillet. Add tomatoes, bay leaf and marjoram; simmer 10 minutes. Add corn and chicken; heat through, mixing well with the sauce.

Per Serving:
264 Calories, 75mg Chol, 18g Carbo, 27g Prot, 138mg Sodium, 10g Fat (2.2g Sat 1.8g Poly 4.8g Mono)

Exchanges: 3 low-fat meat, 1 starch/bread, 1 vegetable

Baked Herbed Chicken

Serve with Quinoa (page 150) and Spaghetti Squash (page 132).

Serves: 4
Cooking time: 25 to 30 minutes
Preparation time: 10 minutes

1 pound boneless skinned chicken breasts
2 teaspoons virgin olive oil
6 tablespoons dry white wine
1/4 cup fresh lemon juice
2 teaspoons dried leaf tarragon
2 teaspoons dried leaf basil
1/2 teaspoon hot red pepper flakes

Preheat the oven to 350F (175C). Trim any fat from chicken breasts and pound lightly between two sheets of waxed paper to flatten. Coat with olive oil and place in a baking dish. Add wine, lemon juice, herbs and pepper flakes, turning chicken to coat both sides. Cover dish with foil. Bake 25 to 30 minutes, until chicken is cooked through.

Per Serving:
177 Calories, 72mg Chol, 1g Carbo, 27g Prot, 68mg Sodium, 5g Fat (1.2g Sat 0.8g Poly 2.5g Mono)
Exchanges: 4 low-fat meat

Chicken à la King

Serve with Broccoli & Pine Nuts (page 115). Noodles or rice can be used instead of toast.

Serves: 4
Cooking time: 20 minutes plus poaching time
Preparation time: 15 minutes

1 teaspoon virgin olive oil
1/4 cup chopped celery
1 cup sliced mushrooms
1-1/2 cups Basic White Sauce (page 10)
2 cups diced cooked chicken (see Poached Chicken, page 63)
1/4 cup drained, chopped canned pimentos
1/4 cup slivered blanched almonds
2 tablespoons dry sherry (optional)
Pepper to taste
4 slices whole-wheat bread, toasted, trimmed

In a large non-stick skillet or saucepan, heat oil. Sauté celery and mushrooms. Add white sauce, chicken and pimentos, stirring to combine, and heat through. Add almonds, sherry and pepper to taste. Cut toast into triangles and spoon chicken over toast.

Per Serving:
324 Calories, 54mg Chol, 29g Carbo, 28g Prot, 355mg Sodium, 11g Fat (2.2g Sat. 2.7g Poly 4.8g Mono)
Exchanges: 2 meat, 2 vegetable, 1 milk

Chicken Rosemary

Guests invariably like the taste and look of this menu so it is at the top of my list for entertaining. Serve with Parsley Potatoes (page 176), Carrots & Zucchini Julienne (page 119) and a salad.

Serves: 4
Cooking time: 40 minutes
Preparation time: 15 minutes

1 broiler-fryer chicken (about 2-1/2 lbs.), cut up
Salt and pepper to taste
4 garlic cloves, crushed
1 teaspoon dried rosemary
1/4 cup dry white wine
1/4 cup Chicken Broth (page 12)

Preheat broiler. Remove skin from chicken. Season chicken with salt and pepper. Place in a broiler pan. Broil 5 minutes on each side until lightly browned; remove from broiler. Place chicken, garlic, rosemary, wine and broth in a large saucepan. Cover and cook over medium heat about 30 minutes or until tender, turning once.

Per Serving:
176 Calories, 75 mg Chol, 1g Carbo, 25g Prot, 130mg Sodium, 6g Fat (1.7g Sat 1.4g Poly 2.3g Mono)
Exchanges: 3 low-fat meat

Chicken Salad

Serve with pita bread toasts and tomato slices.

Serves: 4
Cooking time: 20 minutes (to poach)
Preparation time: 15 minutes

12 ounces Poached Chicken (page 63)
4 green onions, sliced
1 tablespoon dried leaf basil
1 cup plain low-fat yogurt
2 teaspoons tomato paste
1 teaspoon capers and 1 teaspoon caper juice
Pepper to taste
1 bunch watercress
4 large romaine lettuce leaves

Cut chicken diagonally in slices, or in chunks. Place in a medium-size bowl; add green onions and basil. In another bowl, mix the yogurt, tomato paste, capers and caper juice together; season with pepper. Trim tough stems from watercress. Chop 1/4 of the bunch and mix with chicken. Combine chicken and yogurt sauce. Serve over romaine leaves and garnish with remaining watercress.

Per Serving:
175 Calories, 73mg Chol, 5g Carbo, 30g Prot, 148mg Sodium, 3g Fat (1.0g Sat 0.7g Poly 1.1g Mono)

Exchanges: 3 low-fat meat, 1/2 milk

Chicken Tarragon

Serve with Orzo & Pignoli (page 166), and Minted Tomato Sauté (page 139).

Serves: 4
Cooking time: 10 minutes
Preparation time: 15 minutes

1 pound boneless skinned chicken breasts
2 tablespoons low-sodium soy sauce
2 tablespoons water
Juice of 1 lemon
1 teaspoon sesame oil
2 garlic cloves, minced
2 teaspoons dried leaf tarragon
Dash of pepper

Trim any fat from chicken; cut into cubes or thin slices. In a medium-size bowl, combine soy sauce, water, lemon juice and chicken; marinate 15 minutes. In a non-stick skillet or wok, heat oil and cook garlic 1 minute. Add chicken and stir-fry until cooked on all sides. Sprinkle in tarragon and pepper; stir to combine.

Per Serving:
164 Calories, 72mg Chol, 3g Carbo, 27g Prot, 368mg Sodium, 4g Fat (1.0g Sat 1.2g Poly 1.5g Mono)
Exchanges: 4 low-fat meat

Chile Chicken

Serve with Hash Brown Potatoes (page 175).

Serves: 4
Cooking time: 20 minutes
Preparation time: 20 minutes

1 tablespoon virgin olive oil
2 garlic cloves, minced
3 bell peppers (red, green, yellow), cut into strips
2 medium-size onions, sliced
1 teaspoon ground cumin
1-1/2 teaspoons dried leaf oregano
2 teaspoons finely chopped fresh hot chile pepper, or
   1 teaspoon dried hot pepper flakes
12 ounces boneless skinned chicken breasts
3 tablespoons fresh lemon juice
1/4 teaspoon salt
1/2 teaspoon black pepper
2 tablespoons chopped fresh parsley

In a large non-stick skillet, heat oil; add garlic and cook 1 minute. Add bell pepper strips, sliced onions, cumin, oregano and chile. Mix, cover and cook over medium heat 10 minutes. Slice chicken in 1/2-inch strips and sprinkle with lemon juice. Add to vegetables; stir. Cook, covered, over medium heat 10 minutes more, stirring occasionally. Add salt and pepper and garnish with parsley.

Per Serving:
174 Calories, 60mg Chol, 6g Carbo, 23g Prot, 168mg Sodium, 6g Fat (1.2g Sat. 1.0g Poly 3.4g Mono)
Exchanges: 3 low-fat meat, 1 vegetable

Chinese Chicken

Serves: 4
Cooking time: 10 minutes
Preparation time: 20 minutes

12 ounces boneless skinned chicken breasts
1 tablespoon vegetable oil
1 cup broccoli flowerets
1 cup cauliflowerets
1/2 pound mushrooms, sliced
4 green onions, cut in 1-inch pieces
2 tablespoons low-sodium soy sauce
3 tablespoons dry sherry
1 teaspoon grated gingerroot
**1 teaspoon arrowroot dissolved in 2 tablespoons
 water**
1 teaspoon sesame oil
1/4 cup unsalted peanuts

Trim any fat from chicken and thinly slice diagonally. In a large non-stick skillet or wok, heat oil and stir-fry chicken 3 to 4 minutes or until cooked through. Remove with a slotted spoon and keep warm. Add broccoli and cauliflower; stir-fry 2 minutes. Add mushrooms, green onions, soy sauce, sherry and gingerroot; stir-fry 2 minutes. Add dissolved arrowroot, sesame oil, peanuts and chicken. Cook until heated through.

Per Serving:
256 Calories, 72mg Chol, 9g Carbo, 30g Prot, 385mg Sodium, 10g Fat (1.8g Sat. 4.0g Poly 3.3g Mono)
Exchanges: 3-1/2 low-fat meat, 2 vegetable

Cornish Game Hens

Serve with Colcannon (page 173).

Serves: 4
Cooking time: 35 minutes
Preparation time: 15 minutes

2 Cornish game hens (about 1-1/4 lbs. each)
1/4 teaspoon dried dill weed
1/4 teaspoon dried leaf oregano
1/4 teaspoon pepper
Dash paprika
1 tablespoon virgin olive oil
1 garlic clove, minced
2 shallots, minced
1/2 cup vermouth
1 tablespoon frozen orange juice concentrate
1 tablespoon chopped parsley
2 tablespoons slivered blanched almonds

Preheat oven to 350F (175C). Remove skin from hens. Cut each in half, discarding backbones. Season on both sides with the herbs and spices. In a large non-stick skillet, heat oil. Sauté hens about 4 minutes on each side. Transfer to a baking dish. Add garlic and shallots to skillet and sauté about 1 minute. Add vermouth and orange juice and swirl to mix. Pour over hens. Cover dish with foil and bake 20 minutes, basting a few times. Increase oven temperature to 425F (220C), uncover baking dish and bake 5 minutes. Garnish with parsley and almonds.

Per Serving:
220 Calories, 72mg Chol, 8g Carbo, 27g Prot, 49mg Sodium, 5g Fat (0.8g Sat. 0.8g Poly 3.5g Mono)
Exchanges: 3 low-fat meat, 1/2 starch/bread

Crunchy Chicken Bake

Serve with Garlic Cauliflower (page 122), Parsley Potatoes (page 176) and a green salad.

Serves: 6
Cooking time: 50 minutes
Preparation time: 15 minutes

1 broiler-fryer chicken (about 2-1/2 lbs.)
1 cup buttermilk
1/2 teaspoon garlic powder
1/2 teaspoon hot or mild paprika
1/4 teaspoon dried leaf thyme
1/4 teaspoon salt
2 cups finely crushed cereal flakes

Preheat oven to 350F (175C). Coat a 13"x 9" baking dish with non-stick cooking spray. Cut chicken in pieces and remove skin. Rinse and pat dry. Dip chicken pieces in buttermilk. Combine remaining ingredients in a paper or plastic bag. Place chicken in bag, shake until coated and place in baking dish. Bake 50 minutes or until crisp.

Per Serving:
262 Calories, 102mg Chol, 8g Carbo, 35g Prot, 306mg Sodium, 9g Fat (2.5g Sat. 1.9g Poly 3.1g Mono)
Exchanges: 4 low-fat meat, 1/2 starch/bread

Grilled Mustard Turkey Cutlets

Skinned boneless chicken cutlets may also be used for this dish. Serve with Rutabaga Puree (page 133) and a salad.

Serves: 4
Cooking time: 6 minutes
Preparation time: 5 minutes

1 pound turkey breast cutlet, 1/4 inch thick
2 tablespoons Dijon-style mustard
2 tablespoons no-cholesterol, reduced-calorie mayonnaise
1 teaspoon fresh lemon juice
Pepper to taste
Paprika
2 tablespoons chopped fresh parsley

Preheat broiler. Coat broiler pan with non-stick cooking spray. Rinse turkey and pat dry. Mix together mustard, mayonnaise and lemon juice in a small bowl. Coat one side of turkey with half of mustard mixture. Broil about 4 inches from heat source 5 minutes. Turn and coat other side of turkey with mustard mixture and sprinkle with pepper and paprika. Broil 1 minute or until top is browned. Garnish with chopped parsley.

Per Serving:
150 Calories, 74mg Chol, 2g Carbo, 26g Prot, 193mg Sodium, 3g Fat (0.6g Sat 1.5g Poly 0.8g Mono)
Exchanges: 3 low-fat meat

Indian Game Hens

Serve with
Orange Rice
(page 155).

Serves: 4
Cooking time: 40 minutes
Preparation time: 25 minutes

2 Cornish game hens (about 1-1/4 lbs. each)
4 tablespoons soy flour
1/4 teaspoon pepper
3 tablespoons olive oil
4 green onions, chopped
1/2 pound mushrooms, sliced
1 tablespoon plus 1 teaspoon curry powder
Dash red (cayenne) pepper
1/2 cup Chicken Broth (page 12)
1/2 cup plain low-fat yogurt

Cut hens into quarters, remove skin and discard backbone. Place 3 tablespoons of soy flour, pepper and hen pieces in a paper or plastic bag; shake to coat meat. In a large non-stick skillet, heat oil. Add hens and cook about 10 minutes, turning. Reduce heat, cover and cook 20 to 25 minutes, until tender. Remove to a serving platter and keep warm. Sauté green onions and mushrooms in skillet and remove to platter. Reduce heat, add remaining flour, curry powder and cayenne. Cook 1 minute. Stir in broth and blend. Cook 2 minutes or until thickened. Reduce heat and stir in yogurt, blending well. Add more curry to taste if desired. Spoon over hens.

Per Serving:
297 Calories, 101mg Chol, 10g Carbo, 36g Prot, 123mg Sodium, 12g Fat (2.9g Sat. 2.3g Poly 5.6g Mono)
Exchanges: 4 low-fat meat, 2 vegetable

Lemon Chicken Paillards

Serve with Green Peas & Mushrooms (page 131) and Sweet Potato Crisps (page 172).

Serves: 4
Cooking time: 10 minutes
Preparation time: 15 minutes

1 pound boneless skinned chicken breasts, halved
Salt to taste
1/2 teaspoon pepper
2 teaspoons Betty's Butter (page 11)
1/4 cup dry white wine, or Chicken Broth (page 12)
1 garlic clove, minced
2 tablespoons fresh lemon juice
4 lemon slices
2 tablespoons chopped fresh parsley

Place chicken between two sheets of waxed paper and pound to 1/4 inch thickness. Season each side of chicken with salt and pepper. In a large non-stick skillet, heat half of Betty's Butter. Cook chicken over medium-high heat 3 minutes on each side or until cooked through. Remove to a serving dish and keep warm. Add wine to skillet and cook 2 minutes over high heat. Reduce heat, stir in remaining butter, garlic and lemon juice. Spoon juice over chicken; top each chicken piece with a lemon slice and parsley.

Per Serving:
189 Calories, 76mg Chol, 1g Carbo, 26g Prot, 135mg Sodium, 7g Fat (2.1g Sat 2.2g Poly 2.1g Mono)
Exchanges: 3 low-fat meat

Poached Chicken or Turkey

Chicken or turkey breasts can be cut into chunks, sliced thinly on the diagonal or shredded and used in salads or other dishes where precooking is required.

Serves: 4
Cooking time: 10 to 15 minutes
Preparation time: 5 minutes

2 cups Chicken Broth (page 12)
1/2 teaspoon salt
1 bay leaf
Pepper to taste
Pinch celery seeds
1 pound boneless skinned chicken breasts, or turkey breast cutlets

In a deep skillet or large pot, bring broth to a boil. Add seasonings and reduce heat to a simmer. Cook 5 minutes; add chicken or turkey breasts and cook 10 to 15 minutes or until tender and no longer pink in the center. Remove from broth and refrigerate if prepared ahead.

Per Serving:
141 Calories, 72mg Chol, 0g Carbo, 26g Prot, 285mg Sodium, 3g Fat (0.9g Sat 0.7g Poly 1.0g Mono)
Exchanges: 3 low-fat meat

Lime Curry Chicken

This makes a simple and delicious dinner party menu and is one of my favorites to serve visitors. Serve with Raisin Bulgur Pilaf (page 144) and Bok Choy (page 114).

Serves: 4
Cooking time: 15 minutes
Preparation time: 10 minutes

1 pound boneless skinned chicken breasts
2 teaspoons virgin olive oil
2 shallots, thinly sliced
1/4 cup diced green bell pepper
1 tablespoon curry powder
Juice of 2 limes
1/4 cup plain low-fat yogurt
Parsley sprigs
1 tablespoon slivered almonds

Cut chicken diagonally into thin slices. In a large non-stick skillet, heat oil and sauté shallots until softened. Add bell pepper and cook until tender; stir in curry powder. Add chicken and stir-fry until chicken is no longer pink. Add lime juice. Just before serving, stir yogurt into skillet. Garnish with parsley and almonds.

Per Serving:
185 Calories, 72mg Chol, 5g Carbo, 28g Prot, 75mg Sodium, 6g Fat (1.2g Sat 1.0g Poly 3.0g Mono)

Exchanges: 3-1/2 low-fat meat, 1 vegetable

Sesame Chicken

You can use broccoli flowerets if asparagus is unavailable. Serve with Wild Rice (page 159).

Serves: 4
Cooking time: 15 minutes plus poaching time
Preparation time: 10 minutes

12 ounces Poached Chicken (page 63)
1 pound fresh asparagus
4 green onions
1 tablespoon sesame oil
2 garlic cloves, minced
2 tablespoons grated gingerroot
2 tablespoons fresh lime juice
1 tablespoon toasted sesame seeds

Cut chicken into strips about 2 inches long. Snap off ends of asparagus and cut diagonally in 1-inch pieces. Julienne the green onions and steam 4 minutes or until tender; remove from heat. In a non-stick skillet or wok, heat the oil; cook garlic and gingerroot 30 seconds. Add asparagus, green onions, chicken, lime juice and sesame seeds; stir-fry until asparagus is crisp-tender.

Per Serving:
223 Calories, 72mg Chol, 8g Carbo, 30g Prot, 70 mg Sodium, 8g Fat (1.6g Sat 2.8g Poly 3.0g Mono)
Exchanges: 3 low-fat meat, 2 vegetable

Teriyaki Kebabs

Serve with
Asparagus &
Pimento (page
112) and Apple &
Sweet Potatoes
(page 170).

Serves: 4
Cooking time: 6 minutes
Preparation time: 10 minutes plus marinating time

1 pound boneless skinned chicken breasts
2 tablespoons low-sodium soy sauce
2 tablespoons water
1 tablespoon peanut oil
1 tablespoon Dijon-style mustard
2 tablespoons grated gingerroot
2 garlic cloves
1 tablespoon grated orange zest
1/4 cup dry sherry

Cut chicken in cubes. In a medium-size bowl, blend remaining ingredients; add chicken. Marinate at least 1 hour or preferably overnight in the refrigerator. Turn several times. Preheat broiler. Reserving marinade, thread chicken cubes on skewers. Broil about 6 inches from heat source about 3 minutes. Turn and brush with marinade. Continue broiling until all sides are cooked, 2 to 3 minutes more.

Per Serving:
203 Calories, 72mg Chol, 3g Carbo, 27g Prot, 350mg Sodium, 7g Fat (1.5g Sat 1.8g Poly 2.7g Mono)
Exchanges: 3 low-fat meat

Turkey au Poivre

Serve with Rosemary Potatoes (page 178) and Green & Gold Squash (page 136).

Serves: 4
Cooking time: 13 minutes
Preparation time: 10 minutes

1 tablespoon black peppercorns
1 pound turkey breast cutlets, 1/4 inch thick
1 tablespoon whipped butter
1/2 cup dry white wine
1 tablespoon brandy
1 tablespoon chopped parsley

Crush peppercorns in a blender or with a mortar and pestle. Press crushed peppercorns firmly into both sides of turkey cutlet. Pound cutlets with the side of a cleaver to make peppercorns adhere. In a non-stick skillet, heat butter. Cook turkey about 4 minutes on each side. Remove to a warm platter. Add wine and brandy to skillet and bring to a boil, reducing liquid to 1/4 cup. Spoon over the turkey and garnish with parsley.

Per Serving:
158 Calories, 78mg Chol, 1g Carbo, 25g Prot, 68mg Sodium, 3g Fat (1.5g Sat. 0.3g Poly 0.7g Mono)
Exchanges: 3 low-fat meat

Turkey Burgers

Serves: 4
Cooking time: 20 minutes
Preparation time: 10 minutes

1 egg white
1 thin slice whole-wheat bread
1 small onion, grated
1 pound ground turkey
2 teaspoons ground coriander
Salt to taste
1 teaspoon pepper
1/4 teaspoon ground nutmeg
2 teaspoons virgin olive oil

In a large bowl, lightly beat egg white. Tear bread into small pieces; soak in egg white 1 minute. Add remaining ingredients except oil and thoroughly mix. Shape into four patties. In a large non-stick skillet, heat oil. Cook patties over medium heat about 10 minutes on each side until cooked through.

Ready ground turkey usually includes some skin and is therefore not always low in fat. For fat-free turkey, have the butcher grind turkey cutlets or grind them in your own food processor.

Per Serving:
208 Calories, 48mg Chol, 5g Carbo, 17g Prot, 195mg Sodium, 14g Fat (3.7g Sat 3.2g Poly 5.4g Mono)
Exchanges: 3 meat

Turkey Casserole

Serve with Mixed
Green Salad
(page 188).

Serves: 4
Cooking time: 50 minutes
Preparation time: 10 minutes

4 ounces vegetable elbow or shell macaroni
1/2 pound ground turkey
1/4 cup chopped onion
1 garlic clove, minced
1/2 cup tomato sauce
1/2 teaspoon dried leaf thyme
1/4 teaspoon ground cinnamon
1/4 teaspoon salt
Pepper to taste
1/2 cup shredded part-skim mozzarella cheese

Preheat oven to 350F (175C). Cook macaroni until *al dente,* being careful not to overcook. Drain and rinse under cold water. Coat an 8-inch square baking pan or casserole dish with non-stick cooking spray. In a large non-stick skillet, cook turkey, onion and garlic until meat is browned. Drain off fat. Stir in macaroni, tomato sauce, thyme, cinnamon, salt and pepper. Spoon into casserole dish and top with cheese. Bake 30 minutes.

Per Serving:
241 Calories, 40mg Chol, 20g Carbo, 17g Prot, 253mg Sodium, 11g Fat (3.7g Sat 2.1g Poly 3.2g Mono)
Exchanges: 2 meat, 1 starch/bread, 1 vegetable

Turkey Cutlet à l'Oignon

Serve with Almond Rice (page 151).

Serves: 4
Cooking time: 15 minutes
Preparation time: 10 minutes

1 tablespoon virgin olive oil
2 cups sliced onions
1 pound turkey cutlets, 1/4 inch thick
1/4 teaspoon salt
1/2 teaspoon pepper
Paprika
Parsley sprigs
4 cherry tomatoes, halved

In a large non-stick skillet, heat olive oil. Add onions; cook, stirring, about 10 minutes, until tender. Remove with a slotted spoon and keep warm. Sprinkle turkey with salt, pepper and dash of paprika. Brown in skillet over high heat 1 to 2 minutes on each side. Arrange on a platter and top with onions. Garnish with parsley sprigs and tomato halves.

Per Serving:
161 Calories, 72mg Chol, 6g Carbo, 27g Prot, 159mg Sodium, 3g Fat (0.5g Sat 0.4g Poly 1.6g Mono)

Exchanges: 3 low-fat meat, 1 vegetable

Turkey Cutlets Piccata

Serve with Curried Potatoes (page 174) and Nutty Brussel Sprouts (page 116).

Serves: 4
Cooking time: 10 minutes
Preparation time: 10 minutes

1 tablespoon Betty's Butter (page 11)
1 pound turkey cutlets, 1/4 inch thick
1/2 cup Chicken Broth (page 12)
Juice of 1 lemon
Salt and pepper to taste
4 lemon slices
4 parsley sprigs

In a large non-stick skillet, heat butter and sauté cutlets about 3 minutes on each side. Remove to a platter and keep warm. Place broth in skillet with lemon juice; season with salt and pepper and stir. Over medium-high heat, reduce liquid to about 1/3 cup, about 3 minutes. Spoon sauce over turkey and top with lemon slices and parsley.

Per Serving:
144 Calories, 75mg Chol, 2g Carbo, 26g Prot, 113mg Sodium, 4g Fat (1.1g Sat 1.3g Poly 0.9g Mono)
Exchanges: 3 low-fat meat

Turkey Divan

Serves: 4
Cooking time: 10 minutes
Preparation time: 20 minutes

4 cups broccoli flowerets
12 ounces Poached Turkey (page 63)
1-1/2 cups hot Cheese Sauce (page 10)
2 tablespoons grated Parmesan cheese
1 tablespoon slivered blanched almonds

Preheat broiler. Blanch broccoli; rinse under cold water to stop cooking. Diagonally slice turkey. Arrange broccoli in the bottom of a baking dish or casserole and put turkey on top. Cover with Cheese Sauce, sprinkle with grated Parmesan and almonds. Broil 8 to 10 inches from heat source until browned, checking every few minutes.

Per Serving:
285 Calories, 83mg Chol, 20g Carbo, 39g Prot, 375 mg Sodium, 6g Fat (2.5g Sat 1.6g Poly 1.6g Mono)

Exchanges: 4 low-fat meat, 1 milk, 1 vegetable

Turkey Perdue

Serve with
Almond Rice
(page 151).

Serves: 4
Cooking time: 15 minutes
Preparation time: 10 minutes

1 pound turkey breast cutlet, 1/4 inch thick
1 tablespoon virgin olive oil
1 garlic clove, minced
1/2 pound mushrooms, sliced
1/2 lemon, thinly sliced
1 tablespoon soy flour
1/4 teaspoon salt
1/4 teaspoon pepper
1/4 teaspoon dried leaf oregano
1/2 cup vermouth
1 (14-oz.) can whole artichoke hearts, drained, quartered

Cut turkey into 2-inch squares. In a large non-stick skillet, heat oil. Add turkey and cook about 2 minutes on each side. Remove and keep warm. Cook garlic, mushrooms and lemon in same skillet until tender, about 5 minutes. Sprinkle with flour, salt, pepper and oregano. Cook, stirring, 1 minute. Add vermouth and bring to a boil, stirring until thickened. Add artichokes and turkey. Simmer 2 minutes to heat through.

Per Serving:
231 Calories, 72mg Chol, 12g Carbo, 28g Prot, 192mg Sodium,
4g Fat (0.7g Sat. 0.5g Poly 2.6g Mono)
Exchanges: 3 low-fat meat, 2 vegetable

Turkey Stroganoff

Serve with Wild
Rice (page 159)
and Spinach
(page 135).

Serves: 4
Cooking time: 30 to 40 minutes
Preparation time: 15 minutes

1 pound ground lean turkey
1 teaspoon vegetable oil
1 small onion, chopped
2 garlic cloves, minced
1/2 pound fresh mushrooms, sliced
2 tablespoons arrowroot
3/4 cup Chicken Broth (page 12)
3/4 cup white wine
1/4 teaspoon salt
Pinch red (cayenne) pepper
1 teaspoon poppy seeds
1 cup plain low-fat yogurt

In a large non-stick skillet, brown the turkey, about 10 minutes. Drain, remove from pan and keep warm. Heat oil in skillet and cook onion and garlic until softened. Add mushrooms and cook until soft. Stir in arrowroot, broth and wine and bring to a simmer. Stir until sauce thickens. Add salt, pepper and poppy seeds. Return turkey to skillet and simmer, stirring, about 5 minutes. Remove from heat; stir in yogurt.

Per Serving:
320 Calories, 65mg Chol, 12g Carbo, 24g Prot, 241mg Sodium, 17g Fat (4.8g Sat 4.8g Poly 5.4g Mono)

Exchanges: 3 meat, 2 vegetable

Chicken Cacciatore

Serves: 4 as main course
Cooking time: 20 minutes
Preparation time: 20 minutes

3/4 pound boneless skinned chicken breasts
1 teaspoon virgin olive oil
2 garlic cloves, minced
1 medium-size onion, chopped
1 medium-size zucchini, sliced
3 large mushrooms, sliced
1 medium-size green bell pepper, chopped
About 1/2 cup mild tomato salsa
12 ounces spinach spaghetti or linguini

Trim any fat from chicken and slice in thin strips. In a large non-stick skillet, heat oil. Add garlic and onion and sauté until softened. Add chicken slices and cook until they turn white, 5 to 8 minutes. Add vegetables and stir-fry 2 minutes. Add salsa and heat through. Meanwhile, bring a large kettle of water to a boil and cook spaghetti until *al dente,* 8 to 10 minutes. Drain in a colander, turn into a bowl and top with sauce.

Per Serving:
312 Calories, 56mg Chol, 38g Carbo, 25g Prot, 262mg Sodium, 7g Fat (1.5g Sat 1.3g Poly 2.5g Mono)
Exchanges: 2 starch/bread, 2 vegetable, 2 low-fat meat

Omelette Fines Herbes

Serve with Sesame Bread (page 228) and salad. This is a favorite dish of mine for a solo lunch, no more than once a week, or less often if cholesterol is a problem.

Serves: 1
Cooking time: 3 minutes
Preparation time: 5 minutes

1 egg plus 1 egg white
Pepper to taste
1/2 teaspoon vegetable oil
3 tablespoons chopped fresh parsley

In a small bowl, beat eggs about 3 minutes, until frothy. Season with pepper. In a 6-inch non-stick skillet, heat oil. Pour eggs into skillet, sprinkle with parsley and cover. Cook 2 to 3 minutes until puffy. Fold over and turn onto dish.

Per Serving:
117 Calories, 274mg Chol, 1g Carbo, 10g Prot, 119mg Sodium, 8g Fat (2.0g Sat 2.2g Poly 2.8g Mono)
Exchanges: 1 meat, 1/2 fat

Meat

Meat has been the mainstay of the American diet, but in these cholesterol and saturated-fat conscious times, many people are preferring poultry and fish. However, red meat does offer some nutritional benefits. It is important to choose lean cuts, and to trim all visible fat from meat before cooking. Flank steak and round steak are two of the leaner beef cuts.

Today's meat markets do offer 90% lean meat, and natural beef which may be a bit more costly but is raised without antibiotics.

Beef Chop Suey

Serve with
Confetti Rice
(page 153) and
Sesame Spinach
Salad (page 189).

Serves: 4
Cooking time: 12 minutes
Preparation time: 10 minutes

1 pound beef round steak
1 tablespoon vegetable oil
1 teaspoon sesame oil
1 tablespoon low-sodium soy sauce
3 celery stalks, thinly sliced diagonally
2 medium-size onions, sliced
1 cup Chicken Broth (page 12)
2 cups bean sprouts, rinsed

Trim any fat from steak and dice. In a large non-stick skillet or wok, heat oils and stir-fry meat over high heat 1 minute. Stir in soy sauce. Remove meat with a slotted spoon and keep warm. Add the celery, onions and broth to the skillet. Bring to a boil, reduce heat and cook 5 minutes. Add bean sprouts. Cook 3 minutes more, then return meat and stir to heat.

Per Serving:
243 Calories, 64mg Chol, 9g Carbo, 28g Prot, 200mg Sodium, 11g Fat (2.7g Sat 3.0g Poly 3.9g Mono)
Exchanges: 3 meat, 2 vegetables

Broiled Herbed Lamb Chops

Serve with Curried Potatoes (page 174) and Braised Kale (page 128). This is one of my favorite entrees for entertaining. It is quick, tasty and elegant.

Serves: 4
Cooking time: 8 to 10 minutes
Preparation time: 10 minutes

4 (4-oz.) lamb rib chops
2 garlic cloves, minced
1 teaspoon dried leaf rosemary, crushed
Pepper to taste

Preheat broiler. Trim any fat from chops. Mix garlic with rosemary and rub onto chops. Season with pepper. Broil chops 3 inches from heat source 4 to 5 minutes on each side. Lamb is best when served pink, but it can be served well done.

Per Serving:
191 Calories, 81mg Chol, 1g Carbo, 25g Prot, 73mg Sodium, 9g Fat (3.3g Sat 0.5g Poly 4.1g Mono)
Exchanges: 3 meat

Chèvre Burgers

Serve with
Gingered Carrots
(page 121) and
Spicy Couscous
(page 146).

Serves: 4
Cooking time: 6 minutes
Preparation time: 10 minutes

12 ounces 90-percent lean ground beef
1 tablespoon Dijon-style mustard
1/2 teaspoon pepper
1/2 teaspoon garlic salt
1 tablespoon chopped onion
1/2 teaspoon ground coriander
2 tablespoons chopped fresh parsley
3 ounces goat cheese (chèvre)
4 parsley sprigs

Preheat broiler. Mix all ingredients except goat cheese and parsley sprigs together in a medium-size bowl. Cut goat cheese into four equal pieces or rounds. Shape meat mixture into four patties about 3/4 inch thick. Place on a broiler rack. Broil patties 3 inches from heat source 3 minutes. Turn and broil 2 minutes. Place cheese on top of each patty, broil 2 minutes more. Garnish with parsley sprigs.

Per Serving:
279 Calories, 85mg Chol, 1g Carbo, 24g Prot, 269mg Sodium, 17g Fat (7.6g Sat 0.6g Poly 6.8g Mono)
Exchanges: 3 meat

Indian Lamb & Spinach

Serve with Spiced Rice Pilaf (page 157) and a green salad.

Serves: 4
Cooking time: 30 minutes
Preparation time: 15 minutes

1 pound lean lamb
1 pound fresh spinach, trimmed
2 teaspoons virgin olive oil
1 onion, sliced
1 teaspoon ground turmeric
2 teaspoons ground coriander
2 teaspoons ground ginger
1/2 teaspoon chili powder
3 tablespoons low-fat yogurt
1/8 teaspoon dried leaf thyme
1 teaspoon prepared mustard

Trim any fat from lamb and cut into 1-inch cubes. Cut spinach into 1/4-inch strips. In a large non-stick skillet, heat oil and sauté onion until softened. Add lamb, turmeric, coriander, ginger and chili powder. Simmer, stirring, 10 minutes until meat is browned. Stir in spinach and remaining ingredients. Cover and simmer 15 minutes, stirring occasionally. Add water if needed and simmer 15 minutes more, until meat is tender.

Per Serving:
248 Calories, 81mg Chol, 8g Carbo, 29g Prot, 163mg Sodium, 11g Fat (3.6g Sat 0.8g Poly 5.6g Mono)
Exchanges: 3 meat, 1-1/2 vegetable

Mustard London Broil

Serve with Garlic Cauliflower (page 122) and a green salad. This tasty treat is easily prepared, and it can be stretched to serve six.

Serves: 4
Cooking time: 10 minutes
Preparation time: 15 minutes plus 15 minutes marinating time

1 pound beef round steak, about 1 inch thick
1/4 cup Ginger-Soy Marinade (page 200)
1 garlic clove, minced
1 tablespoon chopped fresh parsley
2 tablespoons Dijon-style mustard
1 tablespoon Betty's Butter (page 11)
1/4 teaspoon onion salt
1 tablespoon toasted sesame seeds

Preheat broiler. Trim any fat from steak. Marinate steak 15 minutes, turning frequently to coat. Discard marinade. Mix together remaining ingredients except sesame seeds. Broil steak 3 inches from heat source 4 to 5 minutes on each side for medium rare. Remove from broiler; coat with mixture. Sprinkle with sesame seeds. Slice across grain to serve.

Per Serving:
245 Calories, 66mg Chol, 2g Carbo, 26g Prot, 370mg Sodium, 14g Fat (3.5g Sat 4.4g Poly 4.8g Mono)
Exchanges: 3 meat

Paprika Pork Chops

Serve with a hearty bread and Walnut Watercress Salad (page 192).

Serves: 4
Cooking time: 40 minutes
Preparation time: 15 minutes

4 pork loin chops, about 1/2 inch thick
1 teaspoon vegetable oil
2 medium-size onions, sliced
1-1/4 cups canned Italian plum tomatoes, with liquid
2 teaspoons hot or sweet Hungarian paprika
1 garlic clove, minced
1 teaspoon caraway seeds
4 small new potatoes, thinly sliced
1 small green bell pepper, cut in 1-inch pieces

Trim any fat from pork chops. In a large non-stick skillet, heat oil and brown chops about 5 minutes on each side. Remove and keep warm. In same skillet, sauté onions about 3 minutes. Add tomatoes and liquid, paprika, garlic and caraway seeds. Bring to a boil, reduce heat, cover and simmer 10 minutes. Add potatoes, bell pepper and pork chops; cook 20 minutes.

Per Serving:
313 Calories, 77mg Chol, 22g Carbo, 26g Prot, 315mg Sodium, 14g Fat (4.4g Sat 2.4g Poly 5.7g Mono)
Exchanges: 1 starch/bread, 1 vegetable, 3 meat, 1/2 fat

Pepper Steak

Serve with Parsley Potatoes (page 176) and Bok Choy (page 114).

Serves: 4
Cooking time: 8 minutes
Preparation time: 5 minutes

2 to 3 tablespoons green or black peppercorns
1 pound beef flank steak
1/2 tablespoon olive oil

Preheat broiler. Crack peppercorns in a food processor or blender or with a mortar and pestle. Trim steak of any fat and brush with oil. Sprinkle peppercorns over both sides of steak. Place on a broiler pan and cook 3 inches under heat source 4 minutes. Turn and cook 4 minutes more. Remove from broiler and thinly slice diagonally, across the grain.

Per Serving:
222 Calories, 60mg Chol, 0g Carbo, 22g Prot, 72mg Sodium, 15g Fat (5.7g Sat 0.5g Poly 6.6g Mono)
Exchanges: 3 meat

Rosemary Pork Chops

Serve with Carrot Curry (page 120), Orange Rice (page 155) and Bean Sprouts & Cucumbers (page 181).

Serves: 4
Cooking time: 15 minutes
Preparation time: 5 minutes

4 pork loin chops, about 1/2 inch thick
1/4 teaspoon pepper
2 shallots, chopped
1/2 cup dry sherry
1 teaspoon dried rosemary, crumbled

Trim any fat from pork chops. Heat a large non-stick skillet and brown pork chops on both sides. Sprinkle with pepper and add shallots, sherry and rosemary. Reduce heat to low, cover and simmer 10 minutes until the meat is tender. Serve pork chops with pan juices.

Per Serving:
245 Calories, 77mg Chol, 2g Carbo, 23g Prot, 65mg Sodium, 12g Fat (4.1g Sat 1.4g Poly 5.3g Mono)
Exchanges: 3 meat

Teriyaki Beef and Vegetables

Serve with
Quinoa (page
150).

Serves: 4
Cooking time: 8 to 10 minutes
Preparation time: 15 minutes plus 20 minutes marinating

1 pound beef top round steak
2-1/2 tablespoons low-sodium soy sauce
1 tablespoon sesame oil
2 teaspoons arrowroot
1 tablespoon peanut oil
1 red bell pepper, cut in 1-inch pieces
1 green bell pepper, cut in 1-inch pieces
6 green onions, chopped

Cut steak into thin strips across grain. Mix together the soy sauce, sesame oil and arrowroot; marinate meat in mixture 20 minutes. In a large non-stick skillet or wok, heat peanut oil. Add bell peppers and green onions and stir-fry 3 to 4 minutes. Remove from skillet and keep warm. Stir-fry beef slices 2 to 3 minutes. Combine all ingredients in skillet and stir-fry until hot.

Per Serving:
250 Calories, 69mg Chol, 5g Carbo, 25g Prot, 431mg Sodium, 14g Fat (3.6g Sat 3.0g Poly 6.1g Mono)

Exchanges: 3 meat, 1 vegetable

Veal Marsala

This is excellent with Buckwheat Groats (page 143) and Spicy Collard Greens (page 124).

Serves: 4
Cooking time: 10 minutes
Preparation time: 10 minutes

1 teaspoon virgin olive oil
1 pound veal cutlets
5 green onions, chopped
1/2 cup Marsala wine
3 tablespoons Dijon-style mustard
1/2 cup non-fat yogurt
Pepper to taste
Parsley sprigs

In a large non-stick skillet, heat oil and sauté veal quickly, about 1 minute on each side. Remove from pan and keep warm. Add green onions and wine and bring to a boil. Reduce liquid by half. Stir in remaining ingredients except parsley, and heat through. Return veal to skillet, cook about 4 minutes more until veal is cooked through. Garnish with sauce and parsley.

Per Serving:
315 Calories, 61mg Chol, 6g Carbo, 30g Prot, 224mg Sodium, 17g Fat (6.8g Sat 0.6g Poly 7.2g Mono)
Exchanges: 4 meat, 1 vegetable

Fish & Shellfish

Low in cholesterol and high in healthful omega-3 fish oils, fish offers concentrated protein and is a good choice in meal plans. The speed with which fish and shellfish can be prepared is another advantage. Fish should be purchased from a reliable fish market, preferably on the day it is to be used. When selecting fresh whole fish, look for glistening shiny flesh; it should be sturdy and not limp. If the fish is filleted, the flesh, when poked, should not retain finger indentations. Fish should have a fresh sea flavor. To store, rinse in cold water, pat dry and wrap lightly in foil or plastic wrap. Keep refrigerated until ready to prepare. Fish may be steamed, baked, broiled or sautéed. As a general rule, when baking fish allow 10 minutes per inch of thickness at 450F (230C). Parsley, lemon, tarragon and dill, all complement and add flavor to fish. Marinating fish in soy sauce, buttermilk or lemon juice 15 to 30 minutes before cooking imparts additional flavor.

According to the new ADA exchange method, fish is counted as a low-fat, or lean, meat exchange.

Baked Bluefish

Serve with Orzo & Pignoli (page 166) and Steamed Cabbage (page 118).

Serves: 4
Cooking time: 18 minutes
Preparation time: 10 minutes

1 pound bluefish fillets
1 medium-size red onion, thinly sliced
2 teaspoons virgin olive oil
1 garlic clove, minced
2 tablespoons chopped fresh parsley
Salt and pepper to taste
Paprika
Lemon wedges

Preheat oven to 450F (230C). Coat a 9-inch baking dish with non-stick cooking spray. Rinse fish and pat dry. Arrange onion in the baking dish and top with fish fillets, skin-side down. Mix olive oil, minced garlic and parsley together and spread over fish. Sprinkle with salt and pepper and a little paprika. Bake, uncovered, 18 minutes until fish turns from translucent to opaque. Garnish with lemon wedges.

Per Serving:
254 Calories, 63mg Chol, 3g Carbo, 21g Prot, 129mg Sodium, 17g Fat (3.9g Sat 3.9g Poly 7.5g Mono)

Exchanges: 3 low-fat meat, 1/2 vegetable

Baked Haddock

Serve with Walnut Barley (page 142) and Swiss Chard (page 138).

Serves: 4
Cooking time: 25 to 35 minutes
Preparation time: 15 minutes

1 pound haddock or cod fillets
1/4 cup fresh lemon juice
1/2 teaspoon vegetable oil
2 garlic cloves, minced
1/4 cup Chicken Broth (page 12)
Pepper to taste
4 large mushrooms, sliced
1 medium-size carrot, grated
2 teaspoons dried leaf mint

Preheat oven to 350F (175C). Rinse fish and pat dry. Place fish fillets in a 9-inch casserole dish, add lemon juice and turn fish to coat well. Marinate 10 minutes. In a small non-stick skillet, heat the oil, sauté garlic and then spoon over fish. Add remaining ingredients to casserole dish. Cover with foil and bake 25 to 35 minutes, until fish turns from translucent to opaque.

Per Serving:
112 Calories, 63mg Chol, 3g Carbo, 21g Prot, 82mg Sodium, 2g Fat (0.2g Sat 0.7g Poly 0.3g Mono)
Exchanges: 3 low-fat meat, 1/2 vegetable

Broiled Swordfish

Serve with Hash Brown Potatoes (page 175) and Lemony Summer Squash (page 137).

Serves: 4
Cooking time: 18 minutes
Preparation time: 5 minutes

1/2 bunch watercress
Juice of 1/2 lemon
2 tablespoons plain low-fat yogurt
1/8 teaspoon pepper
Salt to taste
1 pound swordfish, about 1 inch thick
1 tablespoon virgin olive oil (optional)
Dash paprika

Preheat broiler. Mince enough watercress to make 2 tablespoons. Reserve several sprigs for garnish. Mix minced watercress with lemon juice, yogurt, pepper and salt. Brush each side of fish with oil, if desired, and sprinkle with dash of paprika. Broil about 3 inches from heat source 8 minutes; turn and broil 8 to 10 minutes more until fish flakes easily with a fork. Garnish with watercress sprigs and a small amount of the lemon-watercress sauce.

Per Serving:
142 Calories, 44mg Chol, 1g Carbo, 23g Prot, 162mg Sodium, 4g Fat (1.3g Sat 1.0g Poly 0.6g Mono)
Exchanges: 3 low-fat meat

Crispy Fish Fillets

Nice with Sesame Green Beans & Peppers (page 126) and Buckwheat Groats (page 143).

Serves: 4
Cooking time: 10 minutes
Preparation time: 15 minutes

1 pound flounder or sole fillets
1/4 teaspoon salt
1/8 teaspoon pepper
2 tablespoons olive oil
1/3 cup finely crushed cereal flakes
1 lemon, sliced
Parsley sprigs

Preheat oven to 500F (260C). Coat a baking dish with non-stick cooking spray. Rinse fish and pat dry. Season with salt and pepper, then dip in oil. Coat each fillet with crumbs and arrange in prepared baking dish. Bake 10 minutes, until fish turns from translucent to opaque. Garnish with lemon slices and parsley sprigs.

Per Serving:
171 Calories, 57mg Chol, 3g Carbo, 21g Prot, 220mg Sodium, 8g Fat (1.2g Sat 0.9g Poly 5.2g Mono)
Exchanges: 3 low-fat meat, 1/2 fat

Garlic Ginger Mackerel

Serve with Spiced Rice Pilaf (page 157) and Green Peas & Mushrooms (page 131).

Serves: 4
Cooking time: 10 minutes
Preparation time: 10 minutes

1 pound mackerel fillets
1/2 cup fresh lemon juice
2 garlic cloves, minced
2 green onions, chopped
1 teaspoon chopped gingerroot
1 bay leaf
Lemon wedges
Parsley

Rinse fish and pat dry. Cut into four pieces and place in a large non-stick skillet. Combine all remaining ingredients except lemon wedges and parsley and pour over fish. Cover and bring to a boil. Reduce heat and simmer 8 minutes or until fish is tender. Remove bay leaf before serving. Garnish each piece of fish with lemon wedge and parsley.

Per Serving:
231 Calories, 63mg Chol, 2g Carbo, 21g Prot, 75mg Sodium, 15g Fat (3.6g Sat 3.7g Poly 6.0g Mono)
Exchanges: 3 low-fat meat

Herbed Fish Fillets

Serve with Braised Kale (page 128) and Wild Rice (page 159).

Serves: 4
Cooking time: 25 minutes
Preparation time: 10 minutes

3 shallots, chopped
1 pound sole or flounder fillets
1-1/2 teaspoons dried leaf basil, or 3 tablespoons
chopped fresh basil
1/2 teaspoon rosemary, crushed
1/4 teaspoon pepper
1/4 cup vermouth
1/4 cup fresh lemon juice
1 to 2 tablespoons chopped parsley

Preheat oven to 350F (175C). Coat an ovenproof casserole dish with non-stick cooking spray and sprinkle shallots over bottom. Rinse fish and pat dry. Sprinkle each fillet with herbs and pepper. Roll up each fillet starting with widest end. Place in casserole dish side by side. Pour vermouth and lemon juice over fish and bake 25 minutes, until fish turns from translucent to opaque. Garnish with parsley.

Per Serving:
145 Calories, 36mg Chol, 2g Carbo, 23g Prot, 66mg sodium, 2g Fat (0.4g Sat 0.8g Poly 0.8g Mono)
Exchanges: 3 low-fat meat

Mustard Sole Fillets

Serve with
Spaghetti Squash
(page 132) and
Sesame Soba
Noodles (page
167).

Serves: 4
Cooking time: 8 minutes
Preparation time: 10 minutes

1 pound fillet of sole or flounder
2 tablespoons Dijon-style mustard
1 tablespoon no-cholesterol, reduced-calorie
  mayonnaise
Pepper to taste
Lemon wedges
2 tablespoons chopped fresh parsley

Preheat broiler. Coat broiler pan with non-stick cooking spray. Rinse fish and pat dry. Arrange fish on broiler pan. Mix mustard and mayonnaise; spread on top of fish. Season with pepper. Broil fish about 5 inches from heat source 8 minutes. Remove when mustard sauce is bubbling and brown. Garnish with lemon wedges and parsley.

Per Serving:
106 Calories, 57mg Chol, 1g Carbo, 21g Prot, 182 mg Sodium, 2g Fat (0.3g Sat 0.4g Poly 0.3g Mono)
Exchanges: 3 low-fat meat

Sea Bass in Tomato Sauce

Serve with Carrot & Zucchini Julienne (page 119).

Serves: 4
Cooking time: 10 minutes
Preparation time: 10 minutes

1 pound sea bass fillets
Paprika
Salt and black pepper to taste
1 teaspoon olive oil
1 small onion, chopped
1 garlic clove, minced
1/2 green bell pepper, diced
1 celery stalk, diced
6 basil leaves, shredded, or 1/2 teaspoon dried leaf
   basil
1 (8-oz.) can tomato sauce

Preheat broiler. Coat a broiler pan with non-stick cooking spray. Rinse fish and pat dry. Sprinkle with paprika, salt and black pepper. In a non-stick saucepan, heat oil and sauté onion and garlic until softened. Add bell pepper, celery, basil and tomato sauce; bring to a boil. Keep warm. Place fish fillets in a broiler pan and broil about 3 inches from heat source 5 minutes until fish turns from translucent to opaque. Spoon a little of the tomato sauce onto each of 4 plates. Top with a fish fillet and another spoonful of the sauce.

Per Serving:
136 Calories, 58mg Chol, 7g Carbo, 17g Prot, 377mg Sodium, 5g Fat (0.9g Sat 1.1g Poly 2.0g Mono)
Exchanges: 3 low-fat meat, 1 vegetable

Tarragon Salmon Broil

This is an elegant meal and an excellent entertainment offering. Serve with Steamed Cabbage (page 118) and Raisin Bulgur Pilaf (page 144).

Serves: 4
Cooking time: 6 to 8 minutes
Preparation time: 5 minutes

4 salmon steaks, about 1 inch thick
Salt and pepper to taste
1 teaspoon dried leaf tarragon, crushed
4 lemon slices

Preheat broiler. Coat broiler pan with non-stick cooking spray. Rinse salmon and pat dry. Sprinkle with salt and pepper on each side. Place salmon on broiler pan and sprinkle with half the tarragon. Place about 3 inches from heat source and broil 3 to 4 minutes. Turn, sprinkle with remaining tarragon and broil 3 to 4 minutes until fish turns from translucent to opaque. Top each with a lemon slice.

Per Serving:
184 Calories, 75mg Chol, 1g Carbo, 23g Prot, 114mg Sodium, 9g Fat (1.7g Sat 2.1g Poly 4.5g Mono)
Exchanges: 3 low-fat meat

Tasty Tuna Steak

Serve with Buttercup Squash (page 117) and Vegetable Pilaf (page 158).

Serves: 4
Cooking time: 10 minutes
Preparation time: 15 minutes

4 (4-oz.) tuna steaks, 1 inch thick
1/2 cup basil leaves
1 large tomato
1 tablespoon virgin olive oil
Salt and pepper to taste
4 tablespoons shredded part-skim mozzarella cheese
1 lemon, cut in wedges

Preheat broiler. Rinse fish and pat dry. Rinse and dry basil leaves; chop tomato. In a large non-stick skillet, heat oil until it starts to smoke. Reduce heat, place tuna in skillet and brown on both sides. If you like fish rare, cook each side 1 minute, cook about 3 to 5 minutes total to cook through. Remove from pan and top each piece of tuna with a layer of basil leaves and 1/4 of the chopped tomato. Season with salt and pepper and sprinkle with cheese. Broil fish about 3 inches from heat source just until cheese melts. Serve with lemon wedges.

Per Serving:
193 Calories, 48mg Chol, 3g Carbo, 25g Prot, 192mg Sodium, 9g Fat (2.4g Sat 1.4g Poly 4.4g Mono)
Exchanges: 3 low-fat meat, 1/2 vegetable

Teriyaki Monkfish Kebabs

Serve with
Confetti Rice
(page 153) and
Bell Pepper Salad
(page 182).

Serves: 4
Cooking time: 10 minutes
Preparation time: 15 minutes plus 15 minutes marinating

2 tablespoons low-sodium soy sauce
2 tablespoons water
1/4 cup dry sherry
1 teaspoon crystalline fructose
1 garlic clove, crushed
2 teaspoons grated gingerroot
1 green onion, chopped
1 pound monkfish, about 1 inch thick, skin removed
16 cherry tomatoes
1 green bell pepper, cut into 16 (1-inch) cubes

Preheat broiler. Coat broiler pan with non-stick cooking spray. Mix soy sauce, water, sherry, fructose, garlic, gingerroot and green onion in a saucepan. Bring to a boil, then strain into a shallow glass bowl. Cool. Cut fish into 16 pieces, about 2 inches each. Place in a bowl and cover with marinade. Marinate about 15 minutes, turning once, then discard marinade. Alternately thread fish, tomatoes and bell pepper on 8 skewers, using 2 pieces of each per skewer. Place skewers on broiler pan and broil about 3 inches from heat source 3 to 4 minutes. Turn so that fish cooks evenly, and broil 3 minutes more until fish turns from translucent to opaque.

Per Serving:
123 Calories, 74mg Chol, 6g Carbo, 17g Prot, 329mg Sodium, 3g Fat (1.2g Sat 1.0g Poly 1.6g Mono)
Exchanges: 2 low-fat meat, 1 vegetable

Salmon Salad

Serve with Sesame Bread (page 228).

Serves: 4
Cooking time: 10 minutes
Preparation time: 25 minutes

1 pound salmon fillet, skinned
1 tablespoon olive oil
Pepper to taste
1/3 cup chopped green onions
2 tablespoons chopped shallots
1 tablespoon grated gingerroot
1/4 cup red wine vinegar
1 tablespoon low-sodium soy sauce
1 tablespoon fresh lime juice
2 tablespoons dry white wine
3 medium-size heads Belgian endive
1 head radicchio or red leaf lettuce
1 head arugula or watercress
Few sprigs fresh dill
4 teaspoons lumpfish or salmon caviar

Slice salmon into thirds lengthwise. Cut each strip in 1-inch, bite-size pieces. In a large non-stick skillet, heat oil and add salmon; sprinkle with pepper. Add onions, shallots and gingerroot; cook fish 2 minutes on each side, turning once. Stir in vinegar, soy sauce, lime juice and wine. Remove from heat. Meanwhile, cut ends off endive and arrange leaves in a fan shape on a platter. Arrange radicchio between endive and place arugula in the center. Arrange salmon over salad and spoon liquid over salad. Top with dill and caviar.

Per Serving:
252 Calories, 106mg Chol, 4g Carbo, 26g Prot, 302mg Sodium, 14g Fat (2.3g Sat 2.8g Poly 7.3g Mono)
Exchanges: 3 low-fat meat, 1 vegetable

Bouillabaisse

Traditional French bouillabaisse is best eaten looking out over the Mediterranean. Short of that, it makes a special meal for entertaining friends. Serve with Mixed Green Salad (page 188) and Garlic Bread (page 227).

Serves: 6
Cooking time: 35 minutes
Preparation time: 25 minutes

1/2 pound mussels (optional)
1/2 pound medium-size shrimp
1/2 pound halibut or cod fillets
1 teaspoon virgin olive oil
2 shallots, chopped
2 garlic cloves, minced
2-1/2 cups canned Italian plum tomatoes
2 cups clam juice or fish stock
1/2 cup dry white wine
1/2 teaspoon dried leaf basil
1/4 teaspoon dried leaf thyme
1/4 to 1/2 teaspoon hot pepper flakes
1/2 teaspoon pepper
1 bay leaf
1/2 pound bay scallops

Scrub mussels well to rid them of beards and sand. Discard any open ones. Peel and devein shrimp. Cut halibut into bite-size pieces. In a large non-stick saucepan, heat oil. Add shallots and cook until soft. Add garlic and tomatoes, cook, stirring, 1 minute. Add clam juice, wine, basil, thyme, pepper flakes, pepper and bay leaf. Bring to a boil, reduce heat and simmer 15 minutes. Add halibut and simmer 5 minutes. Add shrimp and scallops and cook 5 minutes more. Add mussels, cover pan and simmer about 5 minutes until mussels open, discarding any that do not open. Discard bay leaf.

Per Serving:
203 Calories, 108mg Chol, 12g Carbo, 28g Prot, 584mg Sodium, 3g Fat (0.7g Sat 0.9g Poly 1.0g Mono)
Exchanges: 3 low-fat meat, 2 vegetable

Shrimp Orientale

Serve with Snow Peas & Water Chestnuts (page 134) and Mellow Millet (page 147).

Serves: 4
Cooking time: 30 seconds
Preparation time: 35 minutes plus 15 minutes marinating

1 pound medium-size shrimp
1/2 cup Chicken Broth (page 12)
1 tablespoon grated orange zest
1/4 cup orange juice
2 teaspoons sesame oil
2 garlic cloves, chopped
2 teaspoons grated gingerroot
1/8 teaspoon pepper
2 green onions, chopped

Peel and devein shrimp. Combine all ingredients in a large non-stick skillet and marinate 15 minutes, stirring a few times. Over high heat, bring to a boil. Stir and cook 30 seconds just until shrimp turn pink. Remove shrimp to a serving bowl and spoon sauce over shrimp.

Per Serving:
158 Calories, 174mg Chol, 5g Carbo, 24g Prot, 169mg Sodium, 4g Fat (0.7g Sat 1.7g Poly 1.3g Mono)
Exchanges: 3 low-fat meat, 1 vegetable

Indian Shrimp

Serve with Peppered Potatoes (page 177).

Serves: 6
Cooking time: 25 minutes
Preparation time: 20 minutes

1 pound large shrimp
1 tablespoon virgin olive oil
1 medium-size onion, chopped
2 garlic cloves, minced
4 cups canned Italian plum tomatoes, drained well
2 tablespoons fresh lemon juice
1/2 teaspoon ground coriander
1/4 teaspoon ground ginger
1/8 teaspoon red (cayenne) pepper
1/4 teaspoon ground cumin
Parsley sprigs

Peel and devein shrimp. Rinse and let dry on paper towels. In a large non-stick skillet, heat olive oil. Add onion and garlic and sauté until softened, about 3 minutes. Chop tomatoes and add to skillet with lemon juice and spices. Bring to a boil; reduce heat and simmer, covered, 15 minutes, stirring once to blend. Stir in shrimp and cook 3 to 5 minutes, until pink. Garnish with parsley.

Per Serving:
140 Calories, 116mg Chol, 10g Carbo, 17g Prot, 374mg Sodium, 4g Fat (4g Sat 0.6g Poly 1.9g Mono)

Exchanges: 2 meat, 2 vegetable

Boiled Lobster

This is a special treat I offer myself when dining alone. It is fast, easy and delectable. Serve with Sweet Potato Crisps (page 172) and Colorful Vegetable Salad (page 184).

Serves: 1
Cooking time: 8 minutes
Preparation time: 10 minutes

1 live lobster, about 1-1/4 pounds
Fresh lemon juice
Parsley sprigs

Bring a large kettle of water to a boil. Drop lobster head first into boiling water. Cover and cook 8 minutes. Remove and drain in a colander. Pull claws from lobster and crack thickest part of each. Pour off any liquid. Place lobster stomach up on cutting board and split from head through tip of tail. Arrange claws and halves on serving platter. Drizzle lemon juice over lobster meat and garnish with parsley.

Per Serving:
146 Calories, 103mg Chol, 3.7g Carbo, 29.4g Prot, 92mg Sodium, 0.7g Fat (0.2g Sat 0.1g Poly 0.2g Mono)

Exchanges: 3 low-fat meat

Soft-Shell Crab

Soft-Shell crab are a special seasonal treat. This is one of my favorite entrees when dining alone. Serve with Bean Sprouts & Green Onions (page 113) and Garlic Bread (page 227).

Serves: 1
Cooking time: 6 minutes
Preparation time: 10 minutes

2 to 3 medium-size soft-shell crab
Dash red (cayenne) pepper
1 tablespoon Betty's Butter (page 11)
Juice of 1 lemon
1 tablespoon chopped fresh parsley

Clean crab and lightly dust both sides with cayenne. Heat butter in a large non-stick skillet and sauté crab about 3 minutes on each side. Pour lemon juice over crab, and top with parsley.

Per Serving:
185 Calories, 80mg Chol, 6g Carbo, 16g Prot, 300mg Sodium, 12g Fat (3.1g Sat 4.9g Poly 2.9g Mono)
Exchanges: 3 meat, 1/2 fruit

Crabmeat Salad

Serve with Sesame Bread (page 228), fresh tomatoes and a few spears of cold Asparagus & Pimento (page 112).

Serves: 4
Cooking time: 0
Preparation time: 15 minutes

1 pound fresh lump or backfin crabmeat (imitation crabmeat may be substituted)
1/4 cup plain non-fat yogurt
1/4 cup no-cholesterol, reduced-calorie mayonnaise
1 to 2 tablespoons chopped pimento
1 teaspoon capers
1/8 teaspoon red (cayenne) pepper
4 leaves romaine lettuce or other fresh greens
Paprika
Parsley sprigs

Pick over crabmeat carefully and place in a bowl. Mix yogurt, mayonnaise, pimento, capers and cayenne in a small bowl; toss with crabmeat. Arrange lettuce on 4 plates. Place 1/4 of crabmeat on each plate. Garnish with paprika and parsley sprigs.

Per Serving:
122 Calories, 114mg Chol, 1g Carbo, 24g Prot, 329mg Sodium, 2g Fat (0.3g Sat 0.8g Poly 0.3g Mono)
Exchanges: 3 low-fat meat

Sautéed Sea Scallops

Serve with Risotto (page 156) and Nutty Brussels Sprouts (page 116).

Serves: 4
Cooking time: 10 to 15 minutes
Preparation time: 10 minutes

1 pound sea scallops, sliced horizontally
6 mushrooms, sliced
1/2 green bell pepper, diced
1 medium-size tomato, chopped
1/4 cup dry white wine
2 green onions, chopped
1 teaspoon dried dill weed

Rinse scallops and pat dry. Place mushrooms, bell pepper, tomato and wine in a large non-stick skillet and cook about 5 minutes, until vegetables are tender. Add onions, scallops and dill weed. Cook about 5 minutes, until scallops are opaque.

Per Serving:
120 Calories, 45mg Chol, 3g Carbo, 21g Prot, 233mg Sodium, 1g Fat (0.4g Sat 0.3g Poly 0.3g Mono)
Exchanges: 3 low-fat meat, 1/2 vegetable

Broiled Bay Scallops

Serve with Chile Corn & Peppers (page 123), Avocado & Grapefruit Salad (page 180) and crisp bread.

Serves: 4
Cooking time: 5 minutes
Preparation time: 5 minutes

1 pound bay scallops or sea scallops, halved
1 teaspoon paprika
Pepper to taste
Juice of 1 lemon
2 tablespoons chopped fresh parsley

Preheat broiler. Rinse scallops and pat dry. Place in a baking dish. Season with paprika and pepper on all sides. Sprinkle with lemon juice. Broil scallops about 3 inches from heat source 3 minutes, until they turn opaque. Turn to make certain they are cooked through. Garnish with parsley.

Per Serving:
101 Calories, 45mg Chol, 2g Carbo, 20g Prot, 233mg Sodium, 1g Fat (0.4g Sat 0.3g Poly 0.3g Mono)
Exchanges: 3 low-fat meat

Seafood Newburg

Serve with cooked noodles. Dinner guests will enjoy this out-of-the-ordinary repast.

Serves: 6
Cooking time: 15 minutes
Preparation time: 15 minutes

1/2 pound shrimp
1/2 pound bay scallops
1 tablespoon Betty's Butter (page 11)
1 tablespoon arrowroot
1-1/2 cups evaporated skim milk
Dash pepper
1/4 teaspoon paprika
1/4 teaspoon freshly grated nutmeg
2 tablespoons dry sherry
1/4 cup chopped fresh parsley

Bring a kettle of water to a boil and add shrimp. Cook 1 minute or just until pink. Remove and rinse under cold water. Peel and devein shrimp. Rinse scallops and pat dry. Heat butter in a large non-stick skillet. Add arrowroot and stir to blend. Add a little of the milk to blend, then stir in the remaining milk. Cook, stirring, until the sauce thickens. Add shrimp, scallops and remaining ingredients except parsley; cook until hot. Garnish with parsley.

Per Serving:
138 Calories, 75mg Chol, 9g Carbo, 17g Prot, 221mg Sodium, 3g Fat (0.9g Sat 1.0g Poly 0.7g Mono)
Exchanges: 2 low-fat meat, 1/2 milk

Linguini with Clam Sauce

This is an easy dish to prepare when unexpected guests arrive. Serve with a tossed green salad.

Serves: 4 as main course
Cooking time: 15 minutes
Preparation time: 10 minutes

8 ounces linguini or spinach spaghetti
1 tablespoon virgin olive oil
1 large onion, coarsely chopped
2 large garlic cloves, minced
1/4 cup chopped fresh parsley
1 (10-1/2-oz.) can whole baby clams, with juice
2 tablespoons vodka (optional)
1 tablespoon fresh lemon juice
1 teaspoon dried leaf oregano, crushed
1/2 teaspoon hot pepper flakes
1/4 cup sliced canned water chestnuts, rinsed and
    drained

Bring a large kettle of water to a boil and cook linguini until *al dente,* 10 to 12 minutes. Drain in a colander and set aside. In a large non-stick skillet, heat olive oil. Add onion and garlic and sauté until softened. Add remaining ingredients. Bring to a simmer and cook 5 minutes until heated through. In a serving bowl, toss linguini and sauce.

Per Serving:
327 Calories, 38mg Chol, 47g Carbo, 22g Prot, 69mg Sodium, 5g Fat (0.6g Sat 0.6g Poly 2.6g Mono)

Exchanges: 3 starch/bread, 1-1/2 low-fat meat

Variation: *Red Clam Sauce:* Add 1 cup tomato sauce.

Per Serving:
346 Calories, 38mg Chol, 52g Carbo, 23g Prot, 438mg Sodium, 6g Fat (.6g Sat .7g Poly 2.6g Mono)

Exchanges: 3-1/2 starch/bread, 1-1/2 low-fat meat, 1/2 vegetable

Vegetables

Many fresh vegetables are now available year around in supermarkets, greengrocers and farmer's markets. In most cases, fresh vegetables offer more nutrition than canned or frozen. But sometimes the reverse is true, particularly if produce is not fresh. Frozen peas, kale and collards are good purchases; they have been flash frozen to retain their vitamins and minerals. Neither frozen nor fresh vegetables should be overcooked. Leafy greens should be rinsed thoroughly several times to rid them of sand. Run packages of frozen vegetables under warm water to hasten thawing.

Select produce that is fresh, firm, and brightly colored. Buy produce of uniform size and shape to ensure even cooking. Fresh vegetables lose their nutrients with storage time, so try to purchase just enough to be used for one or two days ahead, and store in the refrigerator before washing. Fresh parsley keeps well when the stems are placed in a glass of water, covered with plastic wrap and refrigerated.

Many vegetables are great eaten raw, just cleaned, cut in bite-size pieces and served with a dip or sauce, or used in a salad.

Asparagus & Pimento

....

Serves: 4
Cooking time: 3 minutes
Preparation time: 10 minutes

1-1/4 pounds fresh asparagus
1 cup water
2 tablespoons fresh lime juice
1/4 cup diced pimento
1 tablespoon toasted pine nuts

Rinse asparagus and snap off tough ends. In a large skillet, bring water to a boil and add asparagus. Cover and steam asparagus until bright green, 2 to 3 minutes. Remove from heat, drain and arrange on a platter. Sprinkle with lime juice; garnish with pimento and pine nuts. Serve warm or chilled.

....

Per Serving:
37 Calories, 0mg Chol, 7g Carbo, 3g Prot, 6mg Sodium, 2g Fat (0.3g Sat 0.7g Poly 0.5g Mono)

Exchanges: 1 vegetable

Bean Sprouts & Green Onions

Serves: 4
Cooking time: 10 minutes
Preparation time: 5 minutes

2 teaspoons walnut oil
1 pound bean sprouts
6 green onions, chopped
1 tablespoon low-sodium soy sauce
1 tablespoon chopped fresh parsley
1 tablespoon sunflower seeds

In a wok or a large, non-stick skillet, heat oil. Rinse bean sprouts under cold water. Sauté green onions about 3 minutes; stir in sprouts to heat through. Toss with soy sauce. Garnish with parsley and sunflower seeds.

Per Serving:
55 Calories, 0mg Chol, 5g Carbo, 2g Prot, 154mg Sodium, 4g Fat (0.4g Sat 2.2g Poly 0.8g Mono)
Exchanges: 1 vegetable, 1 fat

Bok Choy

Serves: 4
Cooking time: 5 minutes
Preparation time: 10 minutes

1 pound bok choy (Chinese celery)
1 teaspoon virgin olive oil
1 garlic clove, minced
1/2 teaspoon crystalline fructose
1 teaspoon low-sodium soy sauce
1 teaspoon sesame oil

Rinse bok choy in cold water. Cut stalks diagonally in 1-inch pieces and leaves into thin shreds. In a large non-stick skillet, heat oil. Add the stems first and sauté, tossing, about 2 minutes. Then add garlic, leaves, fructose, soy sauce and sesame oil, and continue cooking over high heat 2 minutes more.

Per Serving:
40 Calories, 0mg Chol, 5g Carbo, 1g Prot, 59mg Sodium, 2g Fat (0.3g Sat 0.6g Poly 1.3g Mono)
Exchanges: 1 vegetable, 1/2 fat

Broccoli & Pine Nuts

Serves: 4
Cooking time: 5 minutes
Preparation time: 10 minutes

2 pounds fresh broccoli
1 tablespoon Betty's Butter (page 11)
3 tablespoons fresh lime juice
1/4 cup toasted pine nuts (pignoli)

Trim off large stems and cut broccoli into flowerets about 3 inches long. Steam over boiling water until crisp-tender, about 2 minutes. Drain and let dry on paper towels. In a non-stick skillet, heat butter, add lime juice and whisk together. Turn flowerets into skillet and stir-fry 3 minutes. Just before serving, toss with pine nuts.

Per Serving:
106 Calories, 6mg Chol, 6g Carbo, 4g Prot, 33mg Sodium, 8g Fat (1.5g Sat 3.1g Poly 2.4g Mono)

Exchanges: 1 vegetable, 1-1/2 fat

Nutty Brussels Sprouts

Serves: 4
Cooking time: 10 minutes
Preparation time: 10 minutes

1 pound small Brussels sprouts
1 teaspoon virgin olive oil
8 toasted hazelnuts or almonds, chopped
1/8 teaspoon ground cardamom

Wash Brussels sprouts and trim off bottoms of stems and loose leaves. Steam sprouts over boiling water until tender, 7 to 10 minutes. Remove sprouts to a serving bowl and stir in olive oil, nuts and cardamom.

Per Serving:
62 Calories, 0mg Chol, 9.1g Carbo, 3g Prot, 22mg Sodium, 3g Fat (0.4g Sat 0.6g Poly 1.7g Mono)

Exchanges: 1-1/2 vegetable, 1/2 fat

Buttercup Squash

Serves: 4
Cooking time: 15 minutes
Preparation time: 5 minutes

2 medium-size Buttercup squash (about 1-1/2 lbs.)
Ground mace to taste
Pepper to taste

Trim stems off squash and cut each in quarters using a cleaver or large chef's knife to cut, hitting back of knife with a mallet to force it through squash, If necessary. Scrape away seeds. In a large kettle, bring 2 quarts of water to a boil. Add squash sections and cook until tender, 10 to 15 minutes. Remove from water, sprinkle with a little mace and pepper.

Per Serving:
40 Calories, 0mg Chol, 10g Carbo, 1g Prot, 3mg Sodium, 0g Fat
Exchanges: 1 starch/bread

Steamed Cabbage

Serves: 4
Cooking time: 10 minutes
Preparation time: 15 minutes

1 Napa or green cabbage (about 1-1/2 lbs.)
1/4 cup apple cider vinegar
1-1/2 teaspoons crystalline fructose
1/2 teaspoon crushed hot pepper flakes
2 teaspoons caraway seeds
1/4 teaspoon salt
Black pepper to taste
1/4 cup water
1 red bell pepper, diced

Core cabbage and slice thinly. In a small saucepan, mix vinegar, fructose, pepper flakes, caraway seeds, salt, a few dashes of pepper and water; bring to a boil. Cook about 4 minutes and remove from heat. Meanwhile, fill a large kettle with about 1 inch of water and bring to a boil. Place cabbage slices and bell pepper in a steamer basket and place over water. Steam, covered, 3 minutes. Remove to a serving bowl. Pour sauce through a strainer over cabbage and toss well.

Per Serving:
27 Calories, 0mg Chol, 7g Carbo, 1g Prot, 124mg Sodium, 0g Fat
Exchanges: 1 vegetable

Carrot & Zucchini Julienne

Serves: 4
Cooking time: 6 minutes
Preparation time: 15 minutes

1/2 pound carrots
1/2 pound zucchini
1 tablespoon Betty's Butter (page 11)
2 tablespoons fresh lemon juice
Salt and pepper to taste
1 tablespoon poppy seeds

Cut carrots and zucchini into 1/8-inch-thick julienne strips. Place a steamer basket over boiling water and cook carrots, covered, until crisp-tender 3 minutes. Remove to a bowl and keep warm. Steam zucchini, covered, until crisp-tender 1 minute and add to carrots. Heat butter, lemon juice, salt and pepper; stir into vegetables. Sprinkle with poppy seeds and serve.

Per Serving:
47 Calories, 3mg Chol, 6g Carbo, 2g Prot, 108mg Sodium, 3g Fat (0.9g Sat 1.2g Poly 0.8g Mono)
Exchanges: 1 vegetable, 1/2 fat

Carrot Curry

Serves: 4
Cooking time: 25 minutes
Preparation time: 15 minutes

1 pound fresh carrots, cut in 1/2-inch slices
1-1/2 teaspoons crystalline fructose
2 teaspoons lime juice or lemon juice
1 teaspoon Dijon-style mustard
1 teaspoon curry powder
2 teaspoons walnut oil
2 tablespoons raisins
2 tablespoons chopped fresh parsley

In a large saucepan, bring 1 inch of water to a boil. Place carrots in a vegetable steamer over boiling water and cover tightly. Steam 20 minutes and remove from heat. Meanwhile, in a small bowl, mix together fructose, lime or lemon juice, mustard and curry powder. Heat walnut oil in a large skillet, then add carrots and raisins. Toss 2 minutes. Pour the sauce over the carrots and cook, stirring to blend, 2 minutes more. Sprinkle with parsley.

Per Serving:
76 Calories, 0mg Chol, 13g Carbo, 1g Prot, 68mg Sodium, 3g Fat (0.4g Sat 1.5g Poly 0.6g Mono)
Exchanges: 1 vegetable, 1/2 fruit, 1/2 fat

Gingered Carrots

Serves: 4
Cooking time: 15 minutes
Preparation time: 10 minutes

3/4 pound fresh carrots
1/2 cup Chicken Broth (page 12)
Dash onion powder
2 tablespoons fresh lemon juice
1/2 teaspoon ground ginger
1 tablespoon chopped fresh parsley
1 tablespoon whipped butter

Cut carrots in matchstick slices or thin rounds. Place in a saucepan with broth and onion powder. Cook 15 minutes or until tender. Drain, add remaining ingredients and toss lightly.

Per Serving:
56 Calories, 6mg Chol, 9g Carbo, 1g Prot, 51mg Sodium, 2g Fat (1.3g Sat 0.1g Poly 0.6g Mono)
Exchanges: 2 vegetable

Garlic Cauliflower

Serves: 4
Cooking time: 5 minutes
Preparation time: 10 minutes

1 small cauliflower (about 1-1/2 lbs.)
1 tablespoon virgin olive oil
2 large garlic cloves, minced
1 tablespoon toasted sesame seeds
Dash paprika
Pepper to taste

In a large kettle, bring 2 quarts of water to a boil. Trim cauliflower and break into flowerets. Drop into boiling water and cook 2 minutes. Drain in a colander. In a large, non-stick skillet, heat oil and brown garlic. Add cauliflower and sesame seeds and stir-fry 1 minute. Dust with paprika and pepper before serving.

Per Serving:
76 Calories, 0mg Chol, 6g Carbo, 3g Prot, 9mg Sodium, 5g Fat (0.6g Sat 0.9g Poly 2.9g Mono)

Exchanges: 1 vegetable, 1 fat

Chile Corn & Peppers

Serves: 4
Cooking time: 7 minutes
Preparation time: 15 minutes

1 teaspoon vegetable oil
1/2 cup chopped onion
2 cups fresh whole-kernel corn, or 1 (10-oz.) package
** whole-kernel corn, thawed**
1 small red bell pepper, diced
1 small green bell pepper, diced
1/2 teaspoon hot dried chile pepper
1/4 cup tarragon or white wine vinegar

In a large, non-stick skillet, heat oil and cook onion until translucent. Place vegetables in skillet and stir-fry 2 minutes. Stir in chile pepper and vinegar, cooking just long enough to warm through.

Per Serving:
96 Calories, 0mg Chol, 21g Carbo, 3g Prot, 6mg Sodium, 2g Fat (0.2g Sat 0.9g Poly 0.3g Mono)
Exchanges: 1 starch/bread, 1 vegetable

Spicy Collard Greens

Mustard greens, turnip greens or kale may be substituted for collards.

Serves: 4
Cooking time: 30 minutes
Preparation time: 10 minutes

1 pound collard greens
2 cups Vegetable Stock (page 9), or Chicken Broth (page 12)
3 to 4 leaves fresh basil, or 1/2 teaspoon dried leaf basil
2 teaspoons virgin olive oil
3/4 cup chopped onion
2 garlic cloves, minced
1 tablespoon grated gingerroot
1 teaspoon chopped jalapeño pepper
1/4 teaspoon sesame oil
Pepper to taste
1 teaspoon sesame seeds

Rinse greens well in tepid water and slice in thin strips. Place in a saucepan with the stock and basil, cover and cook about 30 minutes, until greens are tender. Heat oil in a non-stick skillet and sauté onion and garlic; stir in gingerroot and jalapeño pepper. Add collards and stir until liquid is nearly evaporated. Add sesame oil and pepper to taste; stir. Sprinkle with sesame seeds.

Per Serving:
56 Calories, 0mg Chol, 7g Carbo, 2g Prot, 28mg Sodium, 3g Fat (0.4g Sat 0.5g Poly 1.7g Mono)
Exchanges: 1 vegetable, 1/2 fat

Braised Endive

Serves: 4
Cooking time: 20 minutes
Preparation time: 10 minutes

1/2 pound Belgian endive, sliced in rings
1 small Red Delicious apple, diced
2 tablespoons fresh lemon juice
2 teaspoons walnut oil
Pinch salt
Pepper to taste
1/2 cup water
2 tablespoons apple cider vinegar
1 tablespoon chopped fresh parsley

Place all ingredients except vinegar and parsley in a large skillet. Cover and bring to a boil. Steam 10 minutes over high heat. Remove cover, cook 2 minutes more until water evaporates. Continue cooking over medium heat 5 minutes. Stir in vinegar. Garnish with parsley.

Per Serving:
50 Calories, 0mg Chol, 7g Carbo, 1g Prot, 44mg Sodium, 3g Fat
(0.4g Sat 1.6g Poly 0.6g Mono)
Exchanges: 1 vegetable, 1/2 fat

Sesame Green Beans & Peppers

Serves: 4
Cooking time: 2 minutes
Preparation time: 15 minutes

1 pound fresh green beans
1 medium-size red bell pepper, cut in 1/4-inch strips
2 tablespoons low-sodium soy sauce
2 tablespoons toasted sesame seeds
1 teaspoon sesame oil

Trim green beans and blanch in boiling water about 2 minutes. Drain and rinse under cold water. Place in a serving bowl with bell pepper and toss with remaining ingredients.

Per Serving:
84 Calories, 0mg Chol, 7g Carbo, 2g Prot, 305mg Sodium, 4g Fat (0.6g Sat 1.7g Poly 1.3g Mono)

Exchanges: 1 vegetable, 1 fat

Artichokes & Green Beans

Serves: 4
Cooking time: 20 minutes
Preparation time: 7 minutes

1/2 pound small Jerusalem artichokes (sunchokes),
  sliced
3/4 pound fresh green beans
2 garlic cloves, minced
2 teaspoons walnut oil
1/2 red bell pepper, diced
2 tablespoons fresh lemon juice
1 tablespoon chopped walnuts
Pepper to taste

Wash and trim artichokes and beans. Bring a large kettle of water to a boil and cook artichokes until tender, about 15 minutes. Add green beans and cook 3 to 4 minutes. Drain and keep warm. Sauté garlic 1 minute in walnut oil, then add bell pepper to warm. Mix all ingredients together and serve.

Per Serving:
124 Calories, 0mg Chol, 20g Carbo, 4g Prot, 6mg Sodium, 4g Fat
(0.5g Sat 2 4g Poly 0.9g Mono)
Exchanges: 1 starch/bread, 1 fat

Braised Kale

Serves: 6
Cooking time: 20 minutes
Preparation time: 15 minutes

2 pounds fresh kale, washed well
1 teaspoon virgin olive oil
1 small onion, chopped
1 garlic clove, minced
1/4 teaspoon pepper
3 tablespoons water
2 teaspoons fresh lemon juice
1 teaspoon imitation bacon bits

Finely chop kale. In a large non-stick skillet, heat oil and sauté onion and garlic until softened. Add kale and remaining ingredients except lemon juice and bacon bits. Cook over medium heat 15 to 20 minutes or until tender, then stir in lemon juice and garnish with bacon bits.

Per Serving:
42 Calories, 0mg Chol, 8g Carbo, 2g Prot, 22mg Sodium, 1g Fat (0.1g Sat 0.2g Poly 0.5g Mono)
Exchanges: 1-1/2 vegetable

Kohlrabi Amandine

Serves: 4
Cooking time: 30 minutes
Preparation time: 10 minutes

1 pound kohlrabi (about 6)
1 tablespoon virgin olive oil
1 tablespoon frozen orange juice concentrate
1/4 cup chopped fresh parsley
1/2 cup Chicken Broth (page 12)
1 tablespoon toasted slivered almonds

Peel and dice kohlrabi. In a large, non-stick skillet, heat oil. Add remaining ingredients except almonds. Cook, covered, 30 minutes until kohlrabi is tender. Drain, uncover and let brown, then serve with sprinkling of almonds.

Per Serving:
66 Calories, 0mg Chol, 7g Carbo, 1g Prot, 13mg Sodium, 4g Fat (0.5g Sat 0.5g Poly 2.9g Mono)
Exchanges: 1 vegetable, 1/2 fat

Leeks Vinaigrette

Serves: 4
Cooking time: 12 minutes
Preparation time: 10 minutes

8 medium-size leeks, trimmed, well washed
1 tablespoon Balsamic Vinaigrette (page 195)

Split the trimmed leeks lengthwise, leaving the white root ends whole. Make certain all sand is rinsed away. Bundle leeks and tie with string. Drop into a saucepan of boiling water and simmer, covered, about 12 minutes, until just tender. Serve immediately with vinaigrette, or place in iced water to stop cooking, and serve chilled.

Per Serving:
76 Calories, 0mg Chol, 8g Carbo, 1g Prot, 46mg Sodium, 5g Fat (0.7g Sat 2.1g Poly 2.3g Mono)
Exchanges: 1 vegetable, 1 fat

Green Peas & Mushrooms

Serves: 4
Cooking time: 10 minutes
Preparation time: 10 minutes

1 cup water
2 cups green peas (fresh or frozen)
1 teaspoon vegetable oil
4 large mushrooms, sliced
3 green onions, chopped
1 tablespoon low-sodium soy sauce

In a saucepan, bring water to a boil, add peas and cook 5 minutes or until just tender. Drain. Meanwhile, heat oil in a non-stick skillet and sauté mushrooms and green onions until tender. Combine with peas and toss with soy sauce.

Per Serving:
80 Calories, 0mg Chol, 13g Carbo, 4g Prot, 221mg Sodium, 2g Fat (0.2g Sat 0.9g Poly 0.3g Mono)
Exchanges: 1 starch/bread

Spaghetti Squash

May be served with tomato sauce, salsa, a grating of Parmesan cheese or a sprinkling of nuts.

Serves: 4
Cooking time: 30 minutes
Preparation time: 5 minutes

1 medium-size spaghetti squash (about 1-1/2 lbs.)
Pepper to taste

Cut squash in half lengthwise. In a kettle of boiling water, cook squash 30 minutes or until squash will separate in strands when probed with a fork. Remove when tender and discard seeds. With a fork, scrape out pulp into a serving dish and sprinkle with pepper.

Per Serving:
23 Calories, 0mg Chol, 5g Carbo, 1g Prot, 1mg Sodium, 0g Fat
Exchanges: 1 vegetable

Rutabaga Puree

Serves: 6
Cooking time: 30 minutes
Preparation time: 15 minutes

1 rutabaga (about 1 lb.), or 1 pound turnips
1 medium-size orange sweet potato
1/4 teaspoon red (cayenne) pepper
1/2 teaspoon freshly grated nutmeg
1/4 cup non-fat dry milk powder
3 tablespoons chopped fresh parsley

Peel and dice rutabaga and sweet potato; place in a saucepan. Cover with water and bring to a boil. Cover and simmer 30 minutes, until tender. Drain, reserving a little of water. Place vegetables in a blender or a food processor fitted with the metal blade and process to a puree. Add cayenne, nutmeg and dry milk; process to blend. Rewarm in saucepan with some of reserved water if necessary. Garnish with parsley and serve.

Per Serving:
55 Calories, 16mg Chol, 12g Carbo, 2g Prot, 32mg Sodium, 0g Fat
Exchanges: 1 vegetable, 1/2 starch/bread

Snow Peas & Water Chestnuts

Serves: 4
Cooking time: 5 minutes
Preparation time: 10 minutes

2 cups fresh snow peas
1 (8-oz.) can (1 cup) sliced water chestnuts
2 teaspoons walnut oil
Dash sesame oil
Salt and pepper to taste

Trim ends and strings off snow peas. Rinse and drain water chestnuts. Dry on paper towel. In a large non-stick skillet or a wok, heat walnut oil and sesame oil. Add snow peas and stir-fry about 2 minutes. Add water chestnuts and stir-fry 2 minutes. Season with salt and pepper.

Per Serving:
99 Calories, 0mg Chol, 10g Carbo, 3g Prot, 60mg Sodium, 3g Fat (0.4g Sat 1.6g Poly 0.7g Mono)
Exchanges: 2 vegetable, 1/2 fat

Spinach

Serves: 4
Cooking time: 7 minutes
Preparation time: 10 minutes

2 pounds fresh spinach
1 teaspoon sesame oil
2 garlic cloves, minced
1 tablespoon toasted sesame seeds

Rinse spinach leaves well and trim off large stems. In a large non-stick skillet, heat sesame oil and sauté garlic. Add wet spinach leaves and cook until wilted, about 5 minutes. Drain; stir in sesame seeds. Serve warm or at room temperature.

Per Serving:
51 Calories, 0mg Chol, 5g Carbo, 4g Prot, 80mg Sodium, 3g Fat (0.4g Sat 1.1g Poly 0.9g Mono

Exchanges: 1 vegetable, 1/2 fat

Green & Gold Squash

Serves: 4
Cooking time: 2 minutes
Preparation time: 10 minutes

1/2 pound zucchini
1/2 pound yellow summer squash
1 garlic clove, minced
1 teaspoon dried leaf oregano
1/4 teaspoon pepper
1 teaspoon virgin olive oil

Slice zucchini and squash in thin rounds. Mix with garlic, oregano and pepper, and place in a steamer basket over boiling water. Cover and steam 2 minutes or until just tender. Remove from basket to serving bowl and toss with oil.

Per Serving:
34 Calories, 0mg Chol, 6g Carbo, 1g Prot, 3mg Sodium, 1g Fat (0.2g Sat 0.2g Poly 0.8g Mono)
Exchanges: 1 vegetable

Lemony Summer Squash

Serves: 4
Cooking time: 5 minutes
Preparation time: 5 minutes

1 pound summer squash
1 tablespoon walnut oil
1 garlic clove, minced
1 teaspoon dried rosemary, crumbled
2 tablespoons fresh lemon juice
Pepper to taste

Slice squash in 1/4-inch rounds. Heat oil in a non-stick skillet and cook garlic 1 minute. Add squash and cook, stirring gently, until tender, about 4 minutes. Stir in remaining ingredients and heat through.

Per Serving:
31 Calories, 0mg Chol, 5g Carbo, 1g Prot, 3mg Sodium, 2g Fat (0.2g Sat 0.9g Poly 0.3g Mono)
Exchanges: 1 vegetable

Swiss Chard

This recipe may be followed for collard greens, turnip or mustard greens, beet tops, spinach and broccoli rabe.

Serves: 4
Cooking time: 10 minutes
Preparation time: 5 minutes

2 pounds fresh Swiss chard
1/8 teaspoon salt
2 teaspoons virgin olive oil
4 lemon wedges
1 tablespoon toasted sesame seeds

Trim chard of any damaged leaves and tough stems. Wash well to remove all sand. In a large saucepan, bring to a boil about 1/2 inch of water and drop in the chard leaves. Return to a boil, cover and cook 2 to 3 minutes until leaves are tender. Add salt and remove from heat. Drain, reserving 1/4 cup of cooking liquid. Chop chard. Add oil to the reserved liquid and pour desired amount over the chard before serving. Serve each portion with a lemon wedge and sesame seeds.

Per Serving:
59 Calories, 0mg Chol, 5g Carbo, 4g Prot, 262mg Sodium, 3g Fat (0.5g Sat 0.4g Poly 1.9g Mono)
Exchanges: 1 vegetable, 1/2 fat

Minted Tomato Sauté

Serves: 4
Cooking time: 5 minutes
Preparation time: 5 minutes

24 cherry tomatoes
1 tablespoon olive oil
1 tablespoon dried leaf mint, or 3 tablespoons
chopped fresh mint

Trim stems from tomatoes and rinse. In a large, non-stick skillet, heat oil. Cook tomatoes 3 minutes, stirring. Add mint and stir to mix.

Per Serving:
47 Calories, 0mg Chol, 4g Carbo, 1g Prot, 8mg Sodium, 4g Fat (0.5g Sat 0.4g Poly 2.5g Mono)

Exchanges: 1 vegetable, 1/2 fat

Rice & Other Grains

In addition to rice, grains such as barley, bulgur wheat, millet, buckwheat (kasha), couscous and the ancient Inca grain, quinoa, are delicious choices. The most popular of these nutritious grains is rice. Brown rice is rich in vitamins, minerals and fiber, but it does take a little longer to cook. The Italian Arborio rice lends itself to risotto and combines nicely with diced vegetables. Basmati is a nutty flavored Indian rice available in white and brown. Long grain rice holds its shape better than short grain, but the short grain makes a creamier rice.

Leftover grains should be covered well and refrigerated and may be used later in soups, casseroles or salads. To reheat, just add 2 to 3 tablespoons of liquid to each cup of grain and simmer 5 minutes in a covered pan. Two or more different leftover grains may be combined.

Wild rice is actually a grass. Millet is a fruit rather than a grain. Each is nutritious and high in fiber.

HOW TO COOK RICE

The proportion of liquid to the rice or grains should be two to one, so that if you are using one cup of rice, two cups of liquid should be used in cooking. For more flavor, use chicken or vegetable broth, or tomato juice for cooking rice. It is best to bring the liquid to a boil before adding the rice. For still more flavor, sauté some onion and garlic in a little olive oil, stir in the rice to coat, then add the boiling liquid. Other vegetables may be added to the rice for color, texture and taste, such as diced green and red bell peppers, zucchini, peas, sliced raddichio, asparagus spears or artichoke hearts. Almonds, pine nuts (pignoli), chopped hazelnuts, walnuts or sesame seeds add texture and crunch. Grains increase in volume 2-1/2 to 3 tImes with cooking.

HINTS FOR FAST-COOKING BROWN RICE

There are a couple of methods to speed up the process of cooking brown rice. One is to soak the rice in water all day, using 2 cups of water per 1 cup of rice. At the end of the day, cook 30 minutes.

Another way is to bring rice and water (same proportions as above) to a boil in the morning. Turn off the heat and let stand, covered, until the evening meal preparation. Using this method, the rice will need to be cooked only 10 minutes.

Soaking the rice at least 2 hours will decrease cooking time to 20 to 30 minutes.

Walnut Barley

Serves: 6
Cooking time: 30 minutes
Preparation time: 10 minutes

1 cup pearl barley
2 cups water
1 cup chopped celery
**1/2 cup chopped walnuts or mixed almonds and
  hazelnuts**
Salt and pepper to taste
2 tablespoons minced fresh parsley

Rinse barley under warm, running water. Let drain. In a medium-size saucepan, bring water to a boil and gradually add barley. Cover and cook 20 to 25 minutes, until tender. Drain in a colander and rinse with warm water. Return barley to saucepan with celery, nuts, salt and pepper; heat through. Garnish with parsley.

Per Serving:
187 Calories, 0mg Chol, 29g Carbo, 5g Prot, 59mg Sodium, 7g Fat (0.6g Sat 4.2g Poly 1.5g Mono)
Exchanges: 2 starch/bread, 1 fat

Buckwheat Groats

Serves: 4 (1-1/8-cup) servings
Cooking time: 25 minutes
Preparation time: 10 minutes

2 teaspoons safflower oil
2 shallots, chopped
1 garlic clove, minced
1 celery stalk, sliced
1/2 cup sliced mushrooms
1 egg white
Pinch salt and pepper
1 cup buckwheat groats (kasha)
2 cups Chicken Broth (page 12)
1 tablespoon pine nuts or sunflower seeds
2 tablespoons chopped fresh parsley

In a non-stick saucepan, heat oil and add vegetables. Cook, stirring, over medium heat about 5 minutes. In a small bowl, beat egg white with salt and pepper. Stir into saucepan. Stir in groats, then add broth and bring to a boil. Reduce heat, cover and cook 10 minutes until tender. When liquid is absorbed, add pine nuts and fluff with a fork. Garnish with parsley.

Per Serving:
116 Calories, 0mg Chol, 18g Carbo, 3g Prot, 64mg Sodium, 4g Fat (0.5g Sat 2.0g Poly 1.1g Mono)
Exchanges: 1 starch/bread, 1/2 fat

Raisin Bulgur Pilaf

Serves: 4
Cooking time: 0
Preparation time: 5 minutes plus 30 minutes soaking

2/3 cup bulgur
2/3 cup boiling water
2 tablespoons golden or dark raisins
1/8 teaspoon salt
1/8 teaspoon ground cumin

Place bulgur in a medium-size bowl and cover with boiling water. Add remaining ingredients and stir to combine. Let stand 30 minutes until water is absorbed. Fluff and serve warm.

Per Serving:
89 Calories, 0mg Chol, 20g Carbo, 3g Prot, 57mg Sodium, 0g Fat
Exchanges: 1 starch/bread

Tropical Bulgur

Serves: 6
Cooking time: 5 minutes
Preparation time: 15 minutes plus 30 minutes soaking

3/4 cup bulgur
3/4 cup boiling water
1 tablespoon vegetable oil
4 tablespoons fresh lime juice
1-1/2 teaspoons ground cumin
1 teaspoon dried leaf oregano
1/4 teaspoon salt
Few dashes red (cayenne) pepper
6 green onions, chopped
1 small red bell pepper, chopped
2 tablespoons chopped fresh parsley
4 romaine lettuce leaves

Place bulgur in a small bowl and cover with boiling water. Let it stand 30 minutes until all liquid is absorbed. In a small bowl, mix oil, lime juice, cumin, oregano, salt and cayenne. Add to bulgur and mix with remaining ingredients except lettuce; fluff with a fork. Refrigerate until chilled. Serve on bed of lettuce leaves.

Per Serving:
109 Calories, 0mg Chol, 19g Carbo, 3g Prot, 78mg Sodium, 3g Fat (0.3g Sat 1.5g Poly 0.6g Mono)
Exchanges: 1 starch/bread, 1/2 fat

Spicy Couscous

Serves: 4
Cooking time: 10 minutes
Preparation time: 10 minutes

1/2 teaspoon vegetable oil
2 green onions, chopped
2 small tomatoes, chopped
1 cup Chicken Broth (page 12)
1 teaspoon olive oil
1/2 teaspoon ground cumin
Pinch salt
1 teaspoon curry powder
1/8 teaspoon ground cinnamon
1 cup couscous
2 tablespoons chopped fresh parsley

In a medium-size non-stick skillet, heat the oil. Add green onions and tomatoes; sauté 3 minutes, stirring. Remove from heat and keep warm. In a medium-size saucepan, combine the remaining ingredients except the couscous and parsley. Cover and bring to a boil. Remove from heat. Add couscous, cover and let stand 5 minutes, until liquid is absorbed. Add tomatoes and green onions and fluff with a fork. Garnish with chopped parsley. Makes 3-1/2 cups.

Per Serving:
121 Calories, 0mg Chol, 21g Carbo, 4.3g Prot, 11mg Sodium, 2g Fat (0.2g Sat 0.5g Poly 1.0g Mono)
Exchanges: 1 starch/bread, 1 vegetable

Mellow Millet

Serves: 4
Cooking time: 30 minutes
Preparation time: 10 minutes

1 cup millet, rinsed
2 cups Chicken Broth (page 12)
1/8 teaspoon salt
2 teaspoons sesame oil
1 celery stalk, diced
4 green onions, chopped
1 (8-oz.) can sliced water chestnuts, drained
1 tablespoon low-sodium soy sauce
Pepper to taste
1 tablespoon slivered almonds

In a medium-size non-stick saucepan, toast millet. Add broth and bring to a boil. Reduce heat and simmer until liquid is absorbed, about 25 minutes. Remove from heat and let stand, covered, 5 minutes. In a large non-stick skillet, heat sesame oil. Add celery and green onions; cook 3 minutes, until just tender. Add water chestnuts and soy sauce; heat through. Stir in millet. Season with pepper. Garnish with almonds. Makes 4-1/2 cups or 4 servings.

Per Serving:
127 Calories, 0mg Chol, 22g Carbo, 3g Prot, 217mg Sodium, 3g Fat (0.4g Sat 1.1g Poly 1.4g Mono)

Exchanges: 1 starch/bread, 1 vegetable, 1/2 fat

Corn & Tomato Polenta

Mushrooms or other vegetables may be used instead of corn.

Serves: 6
Cooking time: 25 to 30 minutes
Preparation time: 20 minutes

1 quart water
1/4 teaspoon salt
1 cup yellow cornmeal
1/2 cup tomato sauce
1 teaspoon dried leaf oregano
1/2 cup whole-kernel corn, drained
1/2 teaspoon crushed hot pepper flakes
Pepper to taste

In a heavy, 3-quart saucepan, bring water and salt to a boil. Slowly pour cornmeal into saucepan so that water does not stop boiling, stirring to keep smooth. Reduce heat and simmer 20 to 25 minutes, stirring often until mixture is stiff. Meanwhile, in a small saucepan, heat tomato sauce, oregano, corn, hot pepper flakes and pepper. When cornmeal is stiff, turn half into a serving dish and top with half the sauce. Layer remaining cornmeal and sauce and let rest 5 to 10 minutes. Cut in squares and serve.

Per Serving:
105 Calories, 0mg Chol, 23g Carbo, 3g Prot, 208mg Sodium, 0g Fat
Exchanges: 1-1/2 starch/bread

Quinoa Pilaf

Pronounced keen-wa, quinoa is a mild-flavored grain that was eaten by the Incas. It is now grown in Colorado and New Mexico and is available in natural food stores.

Serves: 4
Cooking time: 30 minutes
Preparation time: 10 minutes

1 cup quinoa
2 cups Chicken Broth (page 12)
1 tablespoon Betty's Butter (page 11)
1 large onion, chopped
2 garlic cloves, chopped
1 tablespoon grated lemon zest
1/2 teaspoon dried leaf thyme
2 tablespoons minced flat-leaf parsley
Salt and pepper to taste

Rinse quinoa in a strainer and remove any debris. Place in a large non-stick saucepan and toast, stirring, until it darkens slightly. Add broth. Bring to a boil, cover, reduce heat and simmer about 20 minutes until tender. In another skillet, heat butter; add onion and garlic and cook until tender, about 3 minutes. Stir in quinoa, lemon zest, thyme, parsley, salt and pepper to taste.

Per Serving:
155 Calories, 3mg Chol, 28g Carbo, 4g Prot, 74mg Sodium, 3g Fat (0.9g Sat 1.2g Poly 0.8g Mono)
Exchanges: 2 starch/bread

Quinoa

Serves: 4
Cooking time: 25 minutes
Preparation time: 5 minutes

2 teaspoons virgin olive oil
2 large garlic cloves, crushed
1 cup quinoa
2 cups Chicken Broth (page 12)

In a large non-stick skillet, heat oil and cook garlic 2 minutes. Rinse quinoa in a strainer and remove any debris. Add to skillet and brown 2 minutes. Add broth and bring to a boil. Reduce heat, cover and simmer about 20 minutes, until tender.

For additional flavor and nutrition, add mushrooms, peas, pimentos or other diced vegetables.

Per Serving:
97 Calories, 0mg Chol, 17g Carbo, 4g Prot, 21mg Sodium, 3g Fat (0.3g Sat 0.2g Poly 1.6g Mono)
Exchanges: 1 starch/bread, 1/2 fat

Almond Rice

Serves: 6
Cooking time: 15 minutes
Preparation time: 5 minutes plus soaking time

1 cup long-grain brown rice
2 cups water
1 teaspoon low-sodium chicken bouillon granules
2 tablespoons slivered almonds or pine nuts
2 tablespoons grated lemon zest

In a medium-size saucepan, bring rice and water to a boil. Turn off heat and let rice stand in water, covered, 6 hours. When ready to cook, add bouillon granules and bring to a boil. Cook 10 minutes until water is absorbed and rice is tender. Drain, if necessary. Add almonds and lemon zest. Let stand a few minutes, then fluff with a fork and serve.

Per Serving:
96 Calories, 0mg Chol, 19g Carbo, 2g Prot, 123mg Sodium, 1g Fat (0.1g Sat 0.2g Poly 0.6g Mono)
Exchanges: 1 starch/bread

Almond Wild Rice

Serves: 4
Cooking time: 40 to 45 minutes
Preparation time: 5 minutes

3/4 cup wild rice
1-1/2 cups Chicken Broth (page 12)
1 teaspoon walnut oil
1 celery stalk, chopped
1/2 cup sliced mushrooms
2 tablespoons toasted slivered almonds

In a medium-size saucepan, bring rice and broth to a boil. Reduce heat and simmer, covered, 35 minutes or until rice is tender. Drain, if necessary. Meanwhile, heat walnut oil in a small non-stick skillet and sauté celery and mushrooms about 5 minutes. Fluff rice with a fork and add sautéed vegetables.

Per Serving:
147 Calories, 0mg Chol, 24g Carbo, 5g Prot, 10mg Sodium, 4g Fat (0.5g Sat 1.8g Poly 1.5g Mono)

Exchanges: 1 starch/bread, 1 vegetable, 1/2 fat

Confetti Rice

Serves: 6
Cooking time: 35 minutes
Preparation time: 10 minutes plus 2 hours soaking time

1 tablespoon virgin olive oil
1 small onion, chopped
3/4 cup brown Basmati rice, soaked 2 hours
1/4 cup dry white wine
1/4 teaspoon dried leaf thyme, crushed
1/8 teaspoon pepper
2 cups Chicken Broth (page 12), or Vegetable Stock
  (page 9)
1 cup frozen green peas, thawed
1/2 cup diced red bell pepper
2 tablespoons grated Parmesan cheese

In a medium-size non-stick saucepan, heat oil and sauté onion until softened. Rinse and drain rice. Add to saucepan and brown. Add wine, thyme, pepper and broth; bring to a boil. Reduce heat, cover and simmer 15 to 20 minutes until rice is tender. Add peas and bell pepper. Cook, stirring occasionally, until all liquid is absorbed, about 5 minutes. Garnish with cheese and serve.

Per Serving:
192 Calories, 1mg Chol, 34g Carbo, 5g Prot, 59mg Sodium, 3g Fat (0.6g Sat 0.3g Poly 1.8g Mono)
Exchanges: 2 starch/bread, 1/2 fat

Curried Rice

Serves: 6
Cooking time: 45 minutes
Preparation time: 10 minutes

2 cups Chicken Broth (page 12)
1 cup brown Basmati rice, well rinsed
2 teaspoons virgin olive oil
1 small onion, chopped
1-1/2 teaspoons curry powder
1 tablespoon raisins
1/2 cup green peas, thawed if frozen
6 hazelnuts, chopped

In a medium-size saucepan, bring broth and rice to a boil. Cover and simmer 40 minutes until water is absorbed and rice is tender. Drain, if necessary. Meanwhile, heat oil in a non-stick skillet and sauté onion until softened. Stir in curry powder. Add onion, raisins and peas to rice and heat through. Garnish with nuts. Makes 2-1/2 to 3 cups or 6 servings.

Per Serving:
128 Calories, 0mg Chol, 23g Carbo, 3g Prot, 13mg Sodium, 3g Fat (0.3g Sat 0.3g Poly 1.9g Mono)

Exchanges: 1-1/2 starch/bread, 1/2 fat

Orange Rice

Serves: 4
Cooking time: 30 minutes
Preparation time: 5 minutes plus soaking time

1 cup brown Basmati rice, rinsed
1-1/2 cups water
2/3 cup orange juice
1 cinnamon stick
6 whole cloves
1/4 teaspoon ground ginger
1 tablespoon golden raisins

Soak rice 30 minutes to 2 hours before cooking; drain. In a medium-size saucepan, combine remaining ingredients. Bring to a boil; reduce heat. Add drained rice. Cook, partially covered, until liquid is absorbed, about 15 minutes. Cover, reduce heat to low and let steam another 15 minutes. Remove from heat and let rest, covered, 5 minutes. Remove cloves and cinnamon stick. Fluff with a fork and serve.

Per Serving:
158 Calories, 0mg Chol, 35g Carbo, 3g Prot, 3mg Sodium, 1g Fat (0g Sat 0g Poly 0g Mono)

Exchanges: 1 starch/bread, 1 fruit

Risotto

This is a basic risotto recipe. Many ingredients may be added, such as green peas, sliced mushrooms, clams or shrimp. Saffron or turmeric may be added for color.

Serves: 4
Cooking time: 25 minutes
Preparation time: 10 minutes

2 teaspoons virgin olive oil
1 small onion, chopped
1 cup Italian Arborio rice
2 cups Vegetable Stock (page 9)
1/4 teaspoon salt
Pepper to taste
2 tablespoons grated Parmesan or Romano cheese

In a medium-size non-stick saucepan, heat oil and sauté onion until tender. Add rice and cook, stirring, 2 to 3 minutes. Add stock and salt. Bring to a boil, cover and simmer 20 minutes. Remove from heat. Turn rice into a warm dish and season with pepper. Garnish with cheese.

Per Serving:
136 Calories, 1mg Chol, 26g Carbo, 3g Prot, 107mg Sodium, 2g Fat (0.5g Sat 0.1g Poly 1.1g Mono)
Exchanges: 2 starch/bread

Spiced Rice Pilaf

Serves: 6
Cooking time: 30 minutes
Preparation time: 5 minutes plus 2 hours soaking

1 cup brown Basmati rice
1 tablespoon vegetable oil
1 small onion, chopped
1 garlic clove, minced
4 whole cloves
1/8 teaspoon salt
2 cups Chicken Broth (page 12)
1 cinnamon stick
1 teaspoon vegetable oil
1 tablespoon raisins
1 tablespoon blanched slivered almonds or pine nuts

Soak rice 2 hours to shorten cooking time. Rinse and drain. In a large non-stick saucepan, heat 1 tablespoon oil and sauté onion and garlic until tender, 2 to 3 minutes. Add cloves and cook 1 minute. Add rice and stir to coat. Add salt, broth and the cinnamon stick. Bring to a boil. Cover, reduce heat and simmer 20 to 25 minutes, until liquid is absorbed. Discard cinnamon stick. Heat 1 teaspoon oil; add raisins and almonds and warm. Mix with rice and serve.

Per Serving:
176 Calories, 0mg Chol, 31g Carbo, 3g Prot, 41mg Sodium, 5g Fat (0.5g Sat 2.0g Poly 1.1g Mono)
Exchanges: 2 starch/bread, 1 fat

Vegetable Pilaf

Try this recipe with other vegetables such as peas, bell peppers, zucchini, raddichio, radishes, green beans, asparagus, etc.

Serves: 6
Cooking time: 30 minutes
Preparation time: 15 minutes plus 2 hours soaking time

1 cup long-grain brown rice
1 tablespoon Betty's Butter (page 11)
1 shallot, minced
2 green onions, chopped
1 carrot, sliced
1/2 cup sliced snow peas
1/2 cup sliced mushrooms
2 tablespoons dry white wine
1-1/2 cups Chicken Broth (page 12), or Vegetable Stock (page 9)
Salt and pepper to taste
2 tablespoons toasted sesame seeds

Soak rice 2 hours to shorten cooking time. Rinse and drain. In a medium-size non-stick saucepan, heat butter and sauté shallot until softened. Add vegetables and sauté about 3 minutes. Add rice to vegetables, stirring to coat. Cook about 2 minutes. Stir in wine and broth; bring to a boil. Reduce heat, cover and simmer about 25 minutes, until rice is tender and liquid is absorbed. Remove from heat and fluff with a fork. Season with salt and pepper. Garnish with sesame seeds.

Per Serving:
182 Calories, 2mg Chol, 31g Carbo, 4g Prot, 127mg Sodium, 4g Fat (0.8g Sat 1.5g Poly 1.1g Mono)
Exchanges: 2 starch/bread, 1 fat

Wild Rice

Sautéed onions or mushrooms may be added for extra flavor.

Serves: 6
Cooking time: 50 minutes
Preparation time: 5 minutes

3/4 cup wild rice
3 cups Vegetable Stock (page 9), or Chicken Broth
  (page 12)
2 tablespoons sunflower seeds (optional)

Thoroughly rinse rice. In a 3-quart saucepan, bring stock to a boil. Add rice, reduce heat, cover and simmer until tender, about 50 minutes. If liquid is not absorbed, cook a little longer, uncovered. Fluff with a fork. Garnish with sunflower seeds, if desired. Makes 3 to 4 cups.

Per Serving:
86 Calories, 0mg Chol, 16g Carbo, 3g Prot, 2mg Sodium, 2g Fat
(0.1g Sat 0.9g Poly 0.3g Mono)
Exchanges: 1 starch/bread

Pasta & Potatoes

Pasta is perfect. It is nutritious, versatile, economical and low in calories, cholesterol and fat. Pasta is a good source of complex carbohydrates, which are absorbed slowly into the blood stream. One cup of cooked pasta has 210 to 220 calories. Most of the recipes in this chapter are meant to be served as accompaniments to entrees. Pasta lends itself to inventiveness; add "cream" based sauces, or seafood, chicken and vegetables to make a delicious all-in-one meal. Leftover pasta is good served cold as a salad or can be reheated by steaming.

Sizes, shapes and pasta ingredients vary. There are hundreds of kinds of pasta from angel hair to ziti. The best dried pasta is usually packaged by the Italian makers and is made from durum wheat, with or without eggs. Whole-wheat pasta and vegetable-flavored pastas provide extra color and nutrients. Wheat-free pasta, made with artichoke flour, is available for people who can't eat regular pasta because of wheat allergies. Oriental noodles made of buckwheat (soba) are interesting and quick cooking.

HOW TO COOK PASTA

Plenty of water is needed for cooking pasta—about 1 quart for every 4 ounces of dry pasta. A little oil added to the water will prevent pasta from sticking together. The water should always be brought to a full boil and the pasta then slipped in gently so the water keeps boiling. Cooking time varies according to the size and shape of the pasta. Very fine angel hair or orzo take about 3 minutes, as does fresh pasta. Test by removing a strand with a fork and tasting for tenderness. The pasta should be chewy but tender, or *al dente.* When cooked, add a cup or two of cold water and drain in a colander. Shake to remove excess water.

Potatoes are a rich source of complex carbohydrates, vitamin C and potassium, as well as a good source of iron, protein, B vitamins and minerals. Since the peel contains much of the potato's nutrients, leaving the skin on not only saves preparation time, but provides a nourishing bonus.

Idaho or Russet potatos are ideal for baking and mashing. The small round red potato, or new potato, is best when boiled or steamed in its skin and is good for slicing in salads. White or Irish potatoes are good for boiling, mashing or roasting. Sweet potatoes are especially healthful, adding valuable beta carotene to its list of nutrients. They are also high in fiber.

Potatoes should be selected for their firmness and smoothness. Avoid potatoes that are wrinkled, green or sprouted. Potatoes will keep for weeks if stored in a cool, dark, unrefrigerated place. Before cooking, scrub well with a brush and cut away any bruised areas, eyes and sprouts.

HOW TO BAKE POTATOES

To oven bake Idaho or Russet potatoes, preheat oven to 400F (205C), pierce a few times with a fork and bake on a rack 40 to 60 minutes, until tender. Top with yogurt and chopped chives, dill weed, or even a dollop of caviar for a special treat.

Baking in a microwave oven is easy, too. Prepare as for oven baking and place in microwave oven. One potato takes 4 to 5 minutes on HIGH, two will take 6 to 7 minutes and four will need 11 to 12 minutes. Let stand 5 minutes.

Cappelini with Herb Spinach

Serves: 6
Cooking time: 15 minutes
Preparation time: 10 minutes

8 ounces angel hair pasta (cappelini)
1 (10-ounce) package frozen spinach, or 1 pound fresh
   spinach
1 tablespoon virgin olive oil
1 onion, chopped
2 tablespoons chopped fresh parsley
1/2 teaspoon dried leaf basil
1/2 teaspoon dried leaf oregano
1/2 teaspoon ground nutmeg
Salt and pepper to taste
2 tablespoons grated Parmesan cheese

Bring a large kettle of water to a boil and cook pasta until *al dente,* 3 minutes. Drain in a colander; set aside. Meanwhile, place frozen spinach in a steamer rack over boiling water until it can be pierced with a fork. If using fresh spinach, steam until slightly wilted. In a non-stick skillet, heat oil and sauté onion until softened. Place spinach, onion, parsley, basil, oregano, nutmeg, salt and pepper in a blender or a food processor fitted with the metal blade, and process to a puree. Place pasta in a serving bowl, toss with sauce and sprinkle with Parmesan cheese.

Per Serving:
169 Calories, 1mg Chol, 29g Carbo, 6g Prot, 97mg Sodium, 3g Fat
(0.7g Sat 0.3g Poly 1.8g Mono)
Exchanges: 2 starch/bread

Fettucini & Mushrooms

Serves: 6
Cooking time: 25 minutes, combined
Preparation time: 10 minutes

8 ounces vegetable-flavored fettucini
3 tablespoons virgin olive oil
2 large garlic cloves, minced
3/4 pound fresh mushrooms, sliced
1/4 cup dry white wine
2 teapoons fresh lemon juice
1/4 to 1/2 teaspoon hot pepper flakes
1/4 teaspoon salt
1/2 teaspoon pepper
1 teaspoon chopped fresh parsley

Bring a large kettle of water to a boil and cook pasta until *al dente,* 10 to 12 minutes. Drain in a colander and set aside. Meanwhile, in a large non-stick skillet, heat 1 teaspoon of the oil and cook garlic about 1 minute. Add mushrooms and cook, stirring, about 5 minutes. Add wine, lemon juice, hot pepper flakes and salt. Bring to a simmer and cook about 10 minutes until liquid has evaporated. Stir in remaining oil, pepper and parsley. Remove from heat, add pasta to sauce in skillet, toss and reheat over low heat.

Per Serving:
202 Calories, 0mg Chol, 28g Carbo, 5g Prot, 151mg Sodium, 7g Fat (0.9g Sat 0.6g Poly 5.0g Mono)
Exchanges: 2 starch/bread, 1 fat

Fusili with Sun-Dried Tomatoes

Serves: 6
Cooking time: 15 minutes
Preparation time: 15 minutes

8 ounces vegetable-flavored fusili or rotelles
1 tablespoon virgin olive oil
1/2 teaspoon hot pepper flakes
2 large garlic cloves, minced
2 green onions, chopped
2 tablespoons sun-dried tomatoes, chopped (available
    in specialty stores)
1 tablespoon chopped gingerroot
1 tablespoon grated orange zest
1 tablespoon tomato paste
1/2 cup drained and chopped canned Italian plum
    tomatoes
1/4 cup Chicken Broth (page 12)
Salt and pepper to taste
2 tablespoons chopped chives
1 teaspoon sesame oil

Bring a large kettle of water to a boil and cook pasta until *al dente,* 8 to 10 minutes. Drain in a colander and set aside. In a large non-stick skillet, heat oil. Add pepper flakes, garlic, green onions, sun-dried tomatoes, gingerroot and orange zest. Stir-fry 1 minute; then add pasta and stir-fry 1 minute more. Add tomato paste, plum tomatoes, broth, salt and pepper. Mix all ingredients well. Cook until heated through. Garnish with chives and drizzle with sesame oil.

....

Per Serving:
185 Calories, 0mg Chol, 32g Carbo, 7g Prot, 121mg Sodium, 4g Fat
(0.4g Sat 0.6g Poly 2.0g Mono)
Exchanges: 2 starch/bread, 1 fat

Orecchiette & Walnuts

Serves: 6
Cooking time: 10 minutes
Preparation time: 10 minutes

8 ounces orecchiette pasta (little ears) or small shells
2 cups broccoli flowerets
1/4 cup drained chopped pimentos
2 tablespoons chopped fresh parsley
3 tablespoons chopped walnuts
2 tablespoons grated Parmesan or Romano cheese
3 tablespoons virgin olive oil

Bring a large kettle of water to a boil and cook pasta until *al dente,* 8 to 10 minutes. Meanwhile, place broccoli in a colander. When pasta is cooked, drain over broccoli. In a large bowl, combine the pimentos, parsley, walnuts, cheese and olive oil. Add pasta and broccoli and toss with sauce.

Per Serving:
201 Calories, 1mg Chol, 27g Carbo, 6g Prot, 50mg Sodium, 8g Fat
(1.2g Sat 2.0g Poly 4.0 Mono)
Exchanges: 1 starch/bread, 2 vegetable, 1 fat

Orzo & Pignoli

Serves: 6
Cooking time: 10 to 15 minutes
Preparation time: 5 minutes

**8 ounces orzo, or other small pasta, such as mini
  shells
1 tablespoon virgin olive oil
3 tablespoons pine nuts (pignoli)
1 tablespoon dried leaf basil
Salt and pepper to taste**

Bring a large kettle of water to a boil and cook orzo until *al
dente*, 3 minutes. Drain in a colander. Meanwhile, in a small,
non-stick skillet, heat oil and stir in pine nuts. Cook until
golden, about 5 minutes. Add basil. Toss with orzo; season
with salt and pepper to taste. Heat through and serve.

Per Serving:
183 Calories, 2mg Chol, 29g Carbo, 6g Prot, 49mg Sodium, 5g Fat
(1.0g Sat 1.8g Poly 1.5g Mono)
Exchanges: 2 starch/bread, 1 fat

Sesame Soba Noodles

Serves: 6
Cooking time: 5 minutes
Preparation time: 10 minutes

8 ounces soba noodles (Japanese buckwheat) or whole-wheat noodles
6 tablespoons Chicken Broth (page 12)
1 garlic clove, minced
1/4 teaspoon gingerroot
1 tablespoon fresh lime juice
2 tablespoons tahini (sesame butter) or peanut butter
1/4 teaspoon ground cumin
1/8 teaspoon chili powder
Dash red (cayenne) pepper
Pinch salt
3 tablespoons warm water
3 green onions, chopped
1 teaspoon toasted sesame seeds

Bring a large kettle of water to a boil and cook noodles until *al dente,* about 5 minutes. Run under cold water for a few seconds, drain, and turn into a serving bowl. Toss with 2 tablespoons of broth. Place in the freezer to chill quickly. In a small bowl, combine garlic, gingerroot, 1 teaspoon of lime juice, tahini, cumin, chili powder, cayenne, salt and water. When pasta is room temperature, toss with sesame sauce until coated. Add remaining lime juice and broth; toss. Garnish with green onions and sesame seeds.

Per Serving:
143 Calories, 0mg Chol, 27g Carbo, 5g Prot, 136mg Sodium, 3g Fat (0.5g Sat 0.9g Poly 1.3g Mono)
Exchanges: 2 starch/bread

Spaghetti with Broccoli Pesto

Serves: 6
Cooking time: 10 minutes
Preparation time: 10 minutes

1/4 pound broccoli flowerets
1/4 cup chopped fresh parsley
2 garlic cloves, minced
2 tablespoons chopped walnuts
2 tablespoons grated Romano cheese
1 tablespoon virgin olive oil
1/4 teaspoon salt
1/8 teaspoon pepper
8 ounces spaghetti or linguini

In a blender or a food processor fitted with the metal blade, place all ingredients except spaghetti and process to a puree. Bring a large kettle of water to a boil and cook spaghetti until *al dente,* about 8 minutes. Drain in a colander, return to the kettle; stir in broccoli sauce and heat to warm.

Per Serving:
184 Calories, 1mg Chol, 29g Carbo, 7g Prot, 100mg Sodium, 5g Fat (0.8g Sat 1.3g Poly 2.2g Mono)

Exchanges: 2 starch/bread, 1 fat

Vermicelli in Lemon Sauce

Serves: 6
Cooking time: 15 minutes
Preparation time: 10 minutes

1/3 cup evaporated skim milk
2 tablespoons whipped butter
8 ounces vermicelli
1/4 cup fresh lemon juice
2 tablespoons grated Romano or Parmesan cheese
2 tablespoons chopped fresh parsley
Lemon zest twists

In a small saucepan, heat milk and butter. Meanwhile, bring a large kettle of water to a boil and cook vermicelli until *al dente,* 8 to 10 minutes. Drain in a colander, rinse with warm water and turn into a serving bowl. Toss with lemon juice, cheese and warm milk. Garnish with parsley and lemon twists.

Per Serving:
184 Calories, 9mg Chol, 30g Carbo, 7g Prot, 82mg Sodium, 4g Fat (2.0g Sat 0.1g Poly 0.9g Mono)

Exchanges: 2 starch/bread, 1 fat

Apple & Sweet Potatoes

Serves: 4
Cooking time: 45 minutes
Preparation time: 15 minutes

4 medium-size sweet potatoes
1 tablespoon whipped butter
2 tablespoons frozen apple juice concentrate
Salt and pepper to taste
1 medium-size apple, peeled and diced
6 whole cloves
Ground nutmeg

Place sweet potatoes in a saucepan and cover with water. Bring to a boil and cook 30 to 40 minutes or until tender. Remove from water, peel and mash. Add butter, apple juice, salt and pepper. Stir in apple, cloves and dash of nutmeg. Place in an ovenproof serving dish and warm in 350F (175C) oven 10 minutes before serving.

Per Serving:
116 Calories, 6mg Chol, 24g Carbo, 1g Prot, 80mg Sodium, 2g Fat (1.3g Sat 0.1g Poly 0.6g Mono)
Exchanges: 1 starch/bread, 1/2 fruit

Balsamic Sweet Potatoes

Serves: 4
Cooking time: 30 to 40 minutes
Preparation time: 5 minutes

4 medium-size sweet potatoes
2 tablespoons balsamic vinegar
Pepper to taste
1 tablespoon chopped fresh parsley

Place potatoes in a large saucepan and cover with water. Bring to a boil and cook potatoes 30 to 40 minutes or until tender. Remove potatoes and peel. Cut in slices 1/2 inch thick and arrange in a serving dish. Sprinkle with balsamic vinegar, pepper and parsley.

Per Serving:
119 Calories, 0mg Chol, 28g Carbo, 2g Prot, 12mg Sodium, 0g Fat
Exchanges: 2 starch/bread

Sweet Potato Crisps

These are perfect as appetizers as well as a vegetable accompaniment.

Serves: 4
Cooking time: 20 minutes
Preparation time: 15 minutes

4 medium-size sweet potatoes
1 to 2 teaspoons walnut oil
2 teaspoons onion powder
2 teaspoons garlic powder
1/2 to 1 teaspoon pepper
1/2 teaspoon hot Hungarian paprika or chili powder

Preheat oven to 450F (230C). Scrub potatoes well and cut in 1/8-inch slices. Coat a non-stick baking sheet with walnut oil and arrange potato slices on it. Combine the seasonings. Sprinkle potatoes with half of the seasonings. Bake 10 minutes. Using a large spatula, turn, sprinkle with remaining seasonings and bake 10 minutes more until crisp. Serve immediately.

Per Serving:
101 Calories, 0mg Chol, 19g Carbo, 1g Prot, 6mg Sodium, 3g Fat (0.3g Sat 1.5g Poly 0.6g Mono)
Exchanges: 1 starch/bread, 1/2 fat

Colcannon

Serves: 4
Cooking time: 35 to 40 minutes
Preparation time: 15 minutes

3/4 pound kale or green cabbage
1 pound potatoes, peeled, quartered
Salt and pepper to taste
1 tablespoon virgin olive oil
1 medium-size onion, chopped
1/2 cup evaporated skim milk

Bring a large saucepan of water to a boil. Wash kale well and trim off tough stems. Drop kale into boiling water and cook, uncovered, about 8 minutes. Drain and squeeze out excess water. Chop fine and set aside. In the same saucepan, cook potatoes in boiling water, covered, 15 minutes. Drain. Place potatoes in a food mill, a blender or a food processor fitted with the metal blade and process to a puree. Combine potatoes with kale and season with salt and pepper. In a small non-stick skillet, heat oil and sauté onion until softened. Add milk to warm. Combine with potatoes and place in an oven-proof serving dish and warm in oven, if necessary.

Per Serving:
125 Calories, 1mg Chol, 20g Carbo, 5g Prot, 108mg Sodium, 4g Fat (0.5g Sat 0.4g Poly 2.5g Mono)

Exchanges: 1 starch/bread, 1 vegetable, 1/2 fat

Curried Potatoes

Serves: 4
Cooking time: 25 minutes
Preparation time: 10 minutes

1 pound small new potatoes, cut in half
1 tablespoon Betty's Butter (page 11)
1 large garlic clove, minced
1 medium-size onion, chopped
1 teaspoon curry powder
1 tablespoon chopped fresh parsley
1 tablespoon fresh lime juice
1/8 teaspoon salt
Dash red (cayenne) pepper

Bring a large saucepan of water to a boil. Add potatoes and cook, covered, 15 to 20 minutes, until tender. Drain in a colander. In a large non-stick skillet, heat butter and sauté garlic and onion until softened. Stir in curry powder. Add parsley, lime juice, salt and cayenne and mix; add potatoes and toss.

Per Serving:
92 Calories, 3mg Chol, 15g Carbo, 2g Prot, 71mg Sodium, 3g Fat (0.9g Sat 1.2g Poly 0.8g Mono)
Exchanges: 1 starch/bread, 1/2 fat

Hash Brown Potatoes

Serves: 4
Cooking time: 20 to 25 minutes
Preparation time: 15 minutes

4 medium-size red or baking potatoes (about 1 lb.)
2 teaspoons virgin olive oil
1 medium-size green bell pepper, diced
1/4 teaspoon salt
Black pepper to taste
2 tablespoons chopped chives

Scrub potatoes well and cut into 1/3-inch cubes. In a large non-stick skillet, heat oil. Stir in potatoes, bell pepper, salt and black pepper. Cover and cook over medium heat, stirring occasionally, until potatoes are cooked through and crisp, 20 to 25 minutes. Stir in chives.

Per Serving:
68 Calories, 0mg Chol, 11g Carbo, 1g Prot, 115 mg Sodium, 2g Fat (0.3g Sat 0.3g Poly 1.5g Mono)
Exchanges: 1 starch/bread

Parsley Potatoes

Serves: 4
Cooking time: 25 minutes
Preparation time: 15 minutes

8 very small new potatoes (about 1 lb.)
1 tablespoon whipped butter
1/4 cup chopped fresh parsley
Salt and pepper to taste

Pare a ring of skin from center of each potato. Place on a steamer rack over boiling water, cover and steam 15 to 20 minutes, until potatoes are tender. Drain. Place butter and parsley in a serving bowl; add potatoes. Season with salt and pepper, toss and serve.

Per Serving:
106 Calories, 6mg Chol, 19g Carbo, 2g Prot, 83mg Sodium, 2g Fat (1.3g Sat 0.1g Poly 0.6g Mono)

Exchanges: 1 starch/bread, 1/2 fat

Peppered Potatoes

Serves: 4
Cooking time: 25 minutes
Preparation time: 5 minutes

2 medium-size Idaho potatoes (about 1 lb.)
2 garlic cloves, minced
6 whole black peppercorns
1/2 cup skim milk
1/4 teaspoon salt
Paprika

Peel potatoes and thinly slice. Place potatoes in a saucepan with garlic and peppercorns; cover with water. Bring to a boil and cook 20 to 25 minutes until potatoes are soft. Drain. Place in a food mill, a blender or a food processor fitted with the metal blade and process to a puree. Return to pan; add milk and salt. Heat, stirring until blended. Garnish with paprika. Makes 2 cups.

Per Serving:
79 Calories, 1mg Chol, 17g Carbo, 3g Prot, 134mg Sodium, 0g Fat
Exchanges: 1 starch/bread

Rosemary Potatoes

Serves: 4
Cooking time: 20 minutes
Preparation time: 5 minutes

1 tablespoon virgin olive oil
2 garlic cloves, minced
1 pound new potatoes
1/4 teaspoon salt
1/4 teaspoon pepper
1 teaspoon dried rosemary, crumbled

In a large non-stick skillet, heat oil. Add garlic and sauté about 5 minutes. Cut potatoes into 1-inch pieces. Add to garlic and sprinkle with salt, pepper and rosemary. Toss. Increase heat to medium, cover and cook about 15 minutes. Remove cover and cook until potatoes are browned, about 4 minutes.

Per Serving:
120 Calories, 0mg Chol, 20g Carbo, 3g Prot, 120mg Sodium, 4g Fat (0.5g Sat 0.3g Poly 2.5g Mono)
Exchanges: 1 starch/bread, 1 fat

Salads

Leafy greens are the basic ingredient of many salads and are available all year in supermarkets and greengroceries. Salad makings should be bright and fresh looking. The deeper the color, the more minerals and vitamins they contain. Leaf lettuce may be green or red tipped. Bibb lettuce, radicchio (a small round head of nearly purple lettuce), romaine or cos, spinach and watercress provide the best nutrients. Belgian endive, arugula or rocket, Boston lettuce, chicory, dandelion, escarole, Chinese cabbage or bok choy and red and green cabbage are excellent for adding diversity to salads. These may be interchanged and combined as desired. Vegetables, raw or blanched, may also be used in infinite combinations to make a salad.

Prepare greens by rinsing in cool water to remove any dirt, cut off tough stems and separate leaves. A salad spin-dryer is most useful for removing water from greens. If one is not available, pat dry the leaves with paper towels. Store rinsed greens in a plastic bag in the refrigerator until ready to use.

Avocado & Grapefruit Salad

Serves: 4
Cooking time: 0
Preparation time: 15

1 medium-size avocado, peeled
1 small pink grapefruit, sectioned
1 small red onion, thinly sliced
4 tablespoons Poppy Seed Sauce (page 213)

Slice avocado into 8 wedges. Arrange equal amounts of avocado and grapefruit on 4 salad dishes and top each with 2 onion slices. Dress each salad with 1 tablespoon sauce.

Per Serving:
137 Calories, 0mg Chol, 12g Carbo, 3g Prot, 17mg Sodium, 10g Fat (1.6g Sat 1.7g Poly 6.1g Mono)

Exchanges: 1 fruit, 2 fat

Bean Sprouts & Cucumbers

Serves: 4
Cooking time: 1 minute
Preparation time: 10 minutes

2 cups bean sprouts
1 cucumber
1 tablespoon apple cider vinegar
1 tablespoon sesame oil
1 tablespoon low-sodium soy sauce
1 tablespoon water
1 tablespoon toasted sesame seeds
Dash chili powder

Blanch sprouts in boiling water 1 minute, drain and let cool. Peel cucumber, cut in half, seed and slice thinly. Mix with sprouts. In a small bowl, mix vinegar, sesame oil, soy sauce and water. Toss with sprouts. Garnish with sesame seeds and a dash of chili powder.

Per Serving:
67 Calories, 0mg Chol, 5g Carbo, 2g Prot, 155mg Sodium, 5g Fat (0.7g Sat 2.0g Poly 1.9g Mono)
Exchanges: 1 vegetable, 1 fat

Bell Pepper Salad

Serves: 4
Preparation time: 20 minutes
Cooking time: 10 minutes

1 medium-size red bell pepper
1 medium-size green bell pepper
1 medium-size yellow bell pepper
1/2 cup Creamy Garlic Dressing (page 197)
1/4 teaspoon black pepper
2 teaspoons capers, rinsed, drained

Preheat broiler. Place bell peppers under broiler and lightly char, turning to grill all sides. Remove from broiler to a paper bag. Close bag and set aside. When peppers cool, peel, core, seed and cut into strips. Arrange peppers on a platter, alternating colors so that they form a petal, and spoon dressing over them. Sprinkle with black pepper. Garnish with capers and serve warm or chilled.

Per Serving:
30 Calories, 0mg Chol, 6g Carbo, 2g Protein, 67mg Sodium, 0g Fat
Exchanges: 1 vegetable

Chickpea Salad

Serves: 4
Cooking time: 0
Preparation time: 10 minutes

1 (15-oz.) can chickpeas (garbanzos)
1 celery stalk, chopped
2 green onions, chopped
1 garlic clove, minced
1/4 teaspoon hot pepper flakes, or to taste
4 tablespoons Tasty Tahini Dressing (page 205)

Rinse chickpeas, drain and place in a bowl. Add celery and green onions. Combine garlic, pepper flakes and dressing. Pour over chickpea mixture and toss.

Per Serving:
129 Calories, 0mg Chol, 20g Carbo, 7g Prot, 320mg Sodium, 3g Fat (0.4g Sat l.2g Poly 0.8g Mono)
Exchanges: 1 starch/bread, 1 low-fat meat

Colorful Vegetable Salad

Serves: 6
Cooking time: 0
Preparation time: 15 to 20 minutes

1 medium-size head red leaf lettuce
1 bunch radishes, sliced
1 carrot, thinly sliced or grated
1 medium-size red bell pepper, diced
3 green onions, chopped
1/2 cup alfalfa sprouts
1/4 cup Creamy Tofu Dressing (page 199)
1 tablespoon toasted pine nuts

Separate lettuce leaves and trim, rinsing well in cool water.
Spin or pat dry, tear in bite-size pieces and place in a large
salad bowl. Add radishes, carrot, bell pepper, green onions
and sprouts. Toss with dressing and garnish with pine nuts.

Per Serving:
51 Calories, 0mg Chol, 7g Carbo, 3g Prot, 77mg Sodium, 3g Fat
(0.3g Sat 1.0g Poly 0.6g Mono)
Exchanges: 1 vegetable, 1/2 fat

Indian Cucumber Salad

....

Serves: 4
Cooking time: 0
Preparation time: 15 minutes

3 medium-size cucumbers
1 cup plain low-fat yogurt
1 tablespoon fresh lemon juice
1 teaspoon ground cumin
1 teaspoon dried mint leaves

Peel cucumbers, cut in half, discard seeds and slice thinly.
Mix remaining ingredients together, add cucumbers and stir
together.

....

Per Serving:
37 Calories, 1mg Chol, 6g Carbo, 3g Prot, 46mg Sodium, 0g Fat (0g
Sat 0g Poly 0g Mono)
Exchanges: 1 vegetable

Kidney Bean Salad

Serves: 4
Cooking time: 0 minutes
Preparation time: 20 minutes

1 (16-oz.) can kidney or pinto beans, rinsed well, drained
1 celery stalk, diced
1 teaspoon chopped dill pickle
2 teaspoons grated onion
1 egg white, hard-cooked, finely chopped
Romaine lettuce leaves
1/4 cup Anchovy Yogurt Dressing (page 194)

Mix first 5 ingredients together lightly. Arrange on lettuce leaves and top with a spoonful of dressing.

Per Serving:
99 Calories, 2mg Chol, 15g Carbo, 5g Prot, 200mg Sodium, 3g Fat (0.3g Sat 1.0g Poly 0.4g Mono)
Exchanges: 1 starch/bread, 1/2 fat

Lentil Vegetable Salad

This salad may be served warm or chilled.

Serves: 6
Cooking time: 30 minutes
Preparation time: 15 minutes

1 cup red lentils
3 cups Chicken Broth (page 12)
1 bay leaf
1/4 teaspoon dried leaf marjoram
1/4 teaspoon dried leaf thyme
1 teaspoon virgin olive oil
1 medium-size carrot, chopped
1 medium-size celery stalk, chopped
2 green onions, chopped
1/4 teaspoon hot pepper flakes (optional)
1/2 cup sliced water chestnuts, rinsed, drained
1/4 cup Balsamic Vinaigrette (page 195)
Romaine lettuce leaves

Rinse lentils and place in a saucepan with broth, bay leaf, marjoram and thyme. Bring to a boil, reduce heat and simmer, uncovered, 30 minutes or until tender. Drain in a colander. Heat oil in a non-stick saucepan and stir-fry vegetables 3 minutes. Add lentils, hot pepper flakes, water chestnuts and vinaigrette. Serve on a bed of lettuce leaves.

Per Serving:
155 Calories, 0mg Chol, 21g Carbo, 9g Prot, 25mg Sodium, 4g Fat (0.5g Sat 1.3g Poly 1.9g Mono)
Exchanges: 1 vegetable, 1 starch/bread, 1 low-fat meat

Mixed Green Salad

Serves: 4
Cooking time: 0
Preparation time: 15 minutes

1 small head Boston or Bibb lettuce
4 green onions, sliced
4 leaves escarole
1 small bunch chicory
1/4 cup Red Pepper Dressing (page 203)

Trim greens and rinse in cool water. Spin or pat dry and tear into bite-size pieces. In a salad bowl, combine all ingredients with dressing and toss to coat.

Per Serving:
23 Calories, 0mg Chol, 5g Carbo, 1g Prot, 20mg Sodium, 0g Fat
Exchanges: 1 vegetable

Sesame Spinach Salad

Serves: 4
Cooking time: 0
Preparation time: 10 minutes

1 pound fresh spinach
1 cup sliced mushrooms
1 tablespoon low-sodium soy sauce
1 tablespoon water
1 tablespoon walnut oil
Few dashes sesame oil
1 tablespoon toasted sesame seeds

Wash spinach thoroughly and trim off tough stems. Spin or pat dry. Mix remaining ingredients together and toss with spinach.

Per Serving:
71 Calories, 0mg Chol, 5g Carbo, 3g Prot, 217mg Sodium, 5g Fat (0.7g Sat 2.9g Poly 1.4g Mono)

Exchanges: 1 vegetable, 1 fat

Summer Salad

Serves: 4
Cooking time: 0
Preparation time: 15 minutes

2 large beefsteak tomatoes, sliced
1 medium-size red onion, sliced
2 tablespoons chopped fresh basil or parsley
Juice of 1 large lemon
2 tablespoons virgin olive oil
Pepper to taste

Arrange tomato slices on salad plates. Layer a few onion rings on top of tomatoes. Sprinkle with basil or parsley and dash of pepper. Mix lemon juice with oil and spoon over each serving.

Per Serving:
66 Calories, 0mg Chol, 9g Carbo, 2g Prot, 15mg Sodium, 4g Fat (0.5g Sat 0.4g Poly 2.5g Mono)
Exchanges: 1 vegetable, 1 fat

Tossed Bean Salad

Serves: 4
Cooking time: 10 minutes
Preparation time: 15 minutes

1/2 pound green beans, trimmed
1/2 pound yellow wax beans, trimmed
1 egg white, hard-cooked
3 tablespoons fresh lemon juice
1 tablespoon virgin olive oil
2 shallots, chopped
Dash red (cayenne) pepper
1 tablespoon chopped dill, or 1/2 teaspoon dried dill

Blanch beans in boiling water 2 minutes. Drain and rinse under cold water. Chop egg white and mix together with the lemon juice, oil, shallots and cayenne. Spoon dressing over beans, toss and garnish with dill.

Per Serving:
82 Calories, 0mg Chol, 11g Carbo, 3g Prot, 19mg Sodium, 4g Fat
(0.5g Sat 0.5g Poly 2.5g Mono)
Exchanges: 2 vegetable, 1 fat

Walnut Watercress Salad

Serves: 4
Cooking time: 0
Preparation time: 10 minutes

1 large bunch watercress
1/2 cup canned sliced water chestnuts, rinsed and drained
2 heads Belgian endive, sliced in rings
2 tablespoons chopped walnuts
1/4 cup Buttermilk Mustard Dressing (page 196)

Trim tough stems from watercress and rinse in cool water. Spin or pat dry. Mix all ingredients together and serve chilled.

Per Serving:
39 Calories, 35mg Chol, 5g Carbo, 1g Prot, 34mg Sodium, 3g Fat (0.2g Sat 1.6g Poly 0.6g Mono)
Exchanges: 1 vegetable, 1/2 fat

Dressings & Sauces

Dressings serve a multitude of purposes. They may be used to marinate fish, chicken or meat; or as a salad dressing or sauce for fresh vegetables, grains or pasta. Many variations are possible and the low-fat way is to use combinations of buttermilk, non-fat yogurt, low-fat cottage cheese, tofu or tomato juice. A wide choice of herbs and seasonings is available, everything from caraway or poppy seeds to tarragon, dill, basil, oregano or garlic. Balsamic and herbed vinegar dressings impart a special flavor.

Delectable sauces can be made with low-fat milk products and winning combinations of herbs and seasonings, fruit, nuts and vegetables. Sauces made with low-fat yogurt, skim milk, part-skim ricotta cheese and low-fat (1%) cottage cheese all add nourishment, extra calcium and interest to salads, grains, desserts, baked goods, fruit and even main dishes. Serve the sauces warm or chilled. Most are low in calories and many are free exchanges.

Anchovy Yogurt Dressing

Excellent dressing for vegetables, pasta, fish or salads.

Serves: 12 (1-tablespoon) servings
Cooking time: 0
Preparation time: 10 minutes

1/2 cup plain low-fat yogurt
1 tablespoon safflower or corn oil
2 tablespoons white wine vinegar
Pinch salt
1/8 teaspoon white pepper
1 garlic clove, minced
2 tablespoons chopped fresh parsley
1 tablespoon anchovy paste
Dash red (cayenne) pepper

Place all ingredients in a blender and process until smooth. Refrigerate to blend flavors; adjust seasoning before serving. Makes about 3/4 cup.

Per Serving:
21 Calories, 2mg Chol, 1g Carbo, 0g Prot, 38mg Sodium, 2g Fat (0.2g Sat 0.8g Poly 0.4g Mono)
Exchanges: free

Balsamic Vinaigrette

Balsamic vinegar is available in specialty food shops.

Serves: 12 (1-tablespoon) servings
Cooking time: 0
Preparation time: 10 minutes

1 tablespoon Dijon-style mustard
1/4 cup balsamic vinegar
2 tablespoons water
2 tablespoons fresh lemon juice
1/4 teaspoon dried leaf tarragon
1 garlic clove, minced
2 tablespoons safflower oil
2 tablespoons virgin olive oil
Salt and pepper to taste

In a jar, combine the mustard, vinegar, water, lemon juice, tarragon and garlic. Shake well to combine. Add oils and shake again. Season with salt and pepper. Chill before serving. Makes about 3/4 cup.

Per Serving:
44 Calories, 0mg Chol, 1g Carbo, 0g Prot, 36mg Sodium, 5g Fat (0.6g Sat 1.7g Poly 2.3g Mono)
Exchanges: 1 fat

Buttermilk Mustard Dressing

Serves: 12 (1-tablespoon) servings
Cooking time: 0
Preparation time: 5 minutes

1/2 cup buttermilk
1/4 cup plain low-fat yogurt
2 teaspoons Dijon-style mustard
1-1/2 tablespoons peeled, seeded and grated
   cucumber
1 green onion, chopped
2 teaspoons chopped fresh parsley
1 teaspoon *each* grated lemon zest and orange zest
Dash white pepper

Blend all ingredients together and chill before serving. Makes about 3/4 cup.

Per Serving:
5 Calories, 0mg Chol, 1g Carbo, 0g Prot, 19mg Sodium, 0g Fat
Exchanges: free

Creamy Garlic Dressing

Sesame oil is available in the oriental section of the supermarket.

Serves: 12 (1-tablespoon) servings
Cooking time: 0
Preparation time: 10 minutes

1/2 cup evaporated skim milk
2 tablespoons fresh lemon juice
2 large garlic cloves, minced
1/4 teaspoon salt
1 teaspoon dried dill weed
1 teaspoon frozen apple juice concentrate
1/4 teaspoon paprika
1/4 teaspoon white pepper
2 dashes sesame oil
Dash red (cayenne) pepper

Place all ingredients in a blender and process until smooth.
Chill before serving. Makes about 3/4 cup.

Per Serving:
11 Calories, 0mg Chol, 2g Carbo, 1g Prot, 50mg Sodium, 0g Fat
Exchanges: free

Creamy Italian Dressing

Serves: 6 (1-tablespoon) servings
Cooking time: 0
Preparation time: 5 minutes

1 tablespoon virgin olive oil
1 tablespoon vegetable oil
4 tablespoons plain low-fat yogurt
1 tablespoon fresh lemon juice
1/4 teaspoon dried leaf oregano
1/8 teaspoon salt
Pepper to taste

Mix all ingredients together and refrigerate. Shake well before using. Makes 1/3 cup.

Per Serving:
46 Calories, 0mg Chol, 1g Carbo, 0g Prot, 43mg Sodium, 5g Fat
(0.6g Sat 1.7g Poly 2.3g Mono)
Exchanges: 1 fat

Creamy Tofu Dressing

Serves: 32 (1-tablespoon) servings
Cooking time: 0
Preparation time: 10 minutes

1 cup firm tofu (bean curd), sliced
1 large garlic clove, minced
2 tablespoons low-sodium soy sauce
Juice of 1 lemon, with pulp
1/4 teaspoon dried leaf oregano
1/4 teaspoon dried leaf marjoram
3 tablespoons balsamic vinegar
2 green onions, chopped
About 1/4 cup water

Place tofu slices in a blender or a food processor fitted with the metal blade. Add remaining ingredients and only as much water as needed to make desired consistency. Process until smooth. Makes 2 cups.

Per Serving:
9 Calories, 0mg Chol, 1g Carbo, 1g Prot, 52mg Sodium, 1g Fat (0.1g Sat 0.3g Poly 0.1g Mono)
Exchanges: free

Ginger-Soy Marinade

Serves: 6 (2-tablespoon) servings
Cooking time: 0
Preparation time: 10 minutes

1/4 cup apple cider vinegar
2 tablespoons low-sodium soy sauce
2 green onions, chopped
1 tablespoon grated gingerroot
1/4 cup frozen orange juice concentrate
2 tablespoons fresh lemon juice

Mix all ingredients together in a small bowl. Use to marinate meat, chicken, fish for an hour or overnight, turning to coat from time to time. Remaining marinade may be used to baste meat while cooking. Makes 3/4 cup.

Per Serving:
22 Calories, 0mg Chol, 6g Carbo, 1g Prot, 202mg Sodium, 0g Fat
Exchanges: free

Italian Dressing

Serves: 8 (1-tablespoon) servings
Cooking time: 0
Preparation time: 5 minutes

1/4 cup Chicken Broth (page 12)
1 tablespoon virgin olive oil
2 tablespoons red wine vinegar
2 teaspoons Dijon-style mustard
1 garlic clove, minced
1/2 teaspoon dried leaf basil
Pinch dried leaf thyme
Salt and pepper to taste

Mix all ingredients together in a small jar and shake well. Chill before serving. Makes 1/2 cup.

Per Serving:
17 Calories, 0mg Chol, 0g Carbo, 0g Prot, 43mg Sodium, 2g Fat (0.2g Sat 0.1g Poly 1.2g Mono)
Exchanges: free

Popeye Pesto

Use as a salad dressing or serve over pasta, warm or chilled.

Serves: 32 (1-tablespoon) servings
Cooking time: 3 minutes
Preparation time: 10 minutes

1 pound fresh spinach, trimmed
1/2 cup plain low-fat yogurt
1/2 cup low-fat (1%) cottage cheese
1/4 cup grated Parmesan cheese
2 tablespoons dried leaf basil
1/4 cup almonds, chopped
2 garlic cloves
1/4 cup fresh parsley, stems removed

Steam spinach lightly in just the water remaining on leaves after rinsing. Drain. In a blender or a food processor fitted with the metal blade, combine spinach and remaining ingredients and process until smooth. Makes about 2 cups.

Per Serving:
16 Calories, 1mg Chol, 1g Carbo, 1g Prot, 38mg Sodium, 1g Fat (0.2g Sat 0.1g Poly 0.3g Mono)
Exchanges: free

Red Pepper Dressing

Serves: 24 (1-tablespoon) servings
Cooking time: 0
Preparation time: 15 minutes

1/2 cup chopped red bell pepper
1/2 medium-size tomato, diced
2 fresh basil leaves, chopped, or 1/2 teaspoon dried
    leaf basil
2 tablespoons chopped onion
Dash dried leaf thyme
Dash red (cayenne) pepper
1 teaspoon walnut oil
2 teaspoons balsamic vinegar
1/2 teaspoon dried leaf tarragon, crushed
Salt and pepper to taste
1/2 cup buttermilk

In a blender or a food processor fitted with the metal blade, process all ingredients except buttermilk to a puree. Add buttermilk and blend. Chill before serving. Makes about 1-1/2 cups.

Per Serving:
5 Calories, 0mg Chol, 1g Carbo, 0g Prot, 9mg Sodium, 0g Fat (0.1g Sat 0.1g Poly 0.1g Mono)
Exchanges: free

Tarragon Vinaigrette

Serves: 6 (1-tablespoon) servings
Cooking time: 0
Preparation time: 5 minutes

1/4 cup Chicken Broth (page 12), or Vegetable Stock (page 9)
1 tablespoon virgin olive oil
1 tablespoon fresh lemon juice
1 tablespoon apple cider vinegar
2 teaspoons Dijon-style mustard
1 garlic clove, minced
1/2 teaspoon dried leaf tarragon, crushed, or to taste
1/4 teaspoon grated lemon zest
Dash fresh ground pepper

In a small jar, mix all ingredients together, shaking well to blend. Makes 1/3 cup.

Per Serving:
23 Calories, 0mg Chol, 1g Carbo, 0g Prot, 22mg Sodium, 2g Fat (0.3g Sat 0.2g Poly 1.7g Mono)
Exchanges: free

Tasty Tahini Dressing

Tahini, also called sesame paste, is available in natural food stores. This is nice on fish, poultry, tofu, omelets or salads.

Serves: 8 (1-tablespoon) servings.
Cooking time: 0
Preparation time: 5 minutes

1/4 cup tahini
6 tablespoons water
2 tablespoons fresh lemon juice
Dash red (cayenne) pepper

Blend all ingredients together with a wire whisk. Makes about 1/2 cup.

Per Serving:
27 Calories, 0mg Chol, 1g Carbo, 1g Prot, 1mg Sodium, 2g Fat (0.3g Sat 1.0g Poly 0.8g Mono)
Exchanges: 1/2 fat

Yogurt Fines Herbes

Serves: 12 (1-tablespoon) servings
Cooking time: 0
Preparation time: 10 minutes

6 tablespoons plain low-fat yogurt
2 tablespoons tarragon vinegar
2 tablespoons low-sodium soy sauce
1 tablespoon chopped herbs, such as fresh basil, parsley or dill
Pinch dried leaf oregano
1/2 teaspoon chopped onion
1 small garlic clove, minced
1/2 teaspoon Dijon-style mustard
Salt and pepper to taste

Mix all ingredients together well. To blend flavors, chill before serving. Makes 3/4 cup.

Per Serving:
4 Calories, 0mg Chol, 1g Carbo, 0g Prot, 126mg Sodium, 0g Fat
Exchanges: free

Salsa

Serves: 16 (2-tablespoon) servings
Cooking time: 0
Preparation time: 10 minutes

1 small onion, chopped
1 small green bell pepper, chopped
1 small red bell pepper, chopped
1 tomato, chopped
1/2 cup fresh lemon or lime juice
Pepper to taste
1 tablespoon chopped fresh basil, or 1 teaspoon dried
  leaf basil
Hot red pepper flakes (optional)

Combine all ingredients in a small bowl. Let stand 20 minutes before serving. Add hot pepper flakes if desired. Makes 2 cups.

Per Serving:
9 Calories, 0mg Chol, 2g Carbo, 0g Prot, 3mg Sodium, 0g Fat
Exchanges: free

Ambassador Sauce

Serve over fish, chicken or salads.

Serves: 20 (1-tablespoon) servings
Cooking time: 0
Preparation time: 5 minutes

1 cup Chicken Broth (page 12)
1/4 cup plain low-fat yogurt
1 tablespoon sesame oil
1 tablespoon capers
1 anchovy fillet

Place all ingredients in a blender or a food processor fitted with the metal blade and process until pureed. Makes about 1-1/4 cups.

Per Serving:
11 Calories, 0mg Chol, 0g Carbo, 0g Prot, 35mg Sodium, 1g Fat (0.2g Sat 0.4g Poly 0.4g Mono)
Exchanges: free

Cranberry-Orange Sauce

Serves: 16 (2-tablespoon) servings
Cooking time: 10 minutes
Preparation time: 5 minutes

1 (12 oz.) package fresh cranberries
3 tablespoons frozen orange juice concentrate
1 teaspoon no-sugar-added raspberry conserve (optional)
1 orange, cut in 8 sections

Rinse cranberries and place in a medium-size saucepan with a small amount of water. Cook over medium heat, stirring in next 2 ingredients, until berries are soft. In a food processor fitted with the metal blade, process half the cranberries and four orange sections. Repeat with remaining cranberries and oranges. Chill before serving. Makes 2 cups.

Per Serving:
21 Calories, 0mg Chol, 5g Carbo, 0g Prot, 0mg sodium, 0g Fat
Exchanges: free

Creamy Mushroom Sauce

Serves: 40 (1-tablespoon) servings
Cooking time: 15 to 20 minutes
Preparation time: 10 minutes

1 tablespoon Betty's Butter (page 11)
1-1/2 tablespoons minced shallots
1/2 teaspoon paprika
2 cups fresh mushrooms, thinly sliced
1 tablespoon arrowroot
1 tablespoon dry sherry or vermouth
3/4 cup evaporated skim milk
1/4 cup water
Pinch salt
Pinch red (cayenne) pepper

Heat butter in a large non-stick skillet. Add shallots; cook until browned. Add paprika and mushrooms. Cook until tender, about 5 minutes. Stir in arrowroot, then sherry. Add milk, water, salt and cayenne. Stir over medium heat until thick. Makes 2-1/2 cups.

Per Serving:
9 Calories, 1mg Chol, 1g Carbo, 12g Prot, 12mg Sodium, 0g Fat (0.1g Sat 0.2g Poly 0.1g Mono)
Exchanges: free

Avocado Dressing

Serves: 32 (1-tablespoon) servings
Cooking time: 0
Preparation time: 10 minutes

1 large ripe avocado
3 tablespoons fresh lemon juice
1/4 cup chopped onion
1 tablespoon seeded, chopped jalapeño chile
1/2 cup plain low-fat yogurt
1/4 cup skim milk
Salt and pepper to taste

Scoop pulp out of avocado and place in a blender or a food processor fitted with the metal blade. Add lemon juice, onion and jalapeño chile and process to blend. Add yogurt, milk and seasonings and process until smooth. Makes 2 cups.

Per Serving:
15 Calories, 0mg Chol, 1g Carbo, 0g Prot, 12mg Sodium, 1g Fat (0.2g Sat 0.2g Poly 0.8g Mono)
Exchanges: free

Lime & Yogurt Sauce

Serves: 8 (1-tablespoon) servings
Cooking time: 0
Preparation time: 5 minutes

2 tablepoons fresh lime juice
2 tablespoons water
1/8 teaspoon salt
Dash fresh ground pepper
1/4 cup plain low-fat yogurt

Combine first four ingredients. Add yogurt and blend. Makes 1/2 cup.

Per Serving:
4 Calories, 1mg Chol, 0g Carbo, 5g Prot, 5mg Sodium, 0g Fat
Exchanges: free

Poppy Seed Sauce

Serve over fresh fruit or fruit and vegetable salads.

Serves: 20 (1-tablespoon) servings
Cooking time: 0
Preparation time: 5 minutes

1 cup plain low-fat yogurt
2 teaspoons grated orange zest
1 teaspoon grated lemon zest
2 tablespoons raspberry (or apple cider) vinegar
1 tablespoon frozen orange juice concentrate
3 tablespoons poppy seeds

In a small bowl, combine all ingredients and stir until well blended. Chill before serving to develop taste. Makes about 1-1/4 cups.

Per Serving:
13 Calories, 0mg Chol, 1g Carbo, 1g Prot, 9mg Sodium, 1g Fat (0.1g Sat 0.4g Poly 0.1g Mono)
Exchanges: free

Red Pepper Sauce

Serve over
chicken or fish.

Serves: 4
Cooking time: 10 minutes
Preparation time: 10 minutes plus cooling time

4 medium-size red bell peppers
1 tablespoon frozen apple juice concentrate
1 teaspoon minced garlic
Salt and pepper to taste

Preheat broiler. Place peppers in broiler about 3 inches from heat source and broil, turning occasionally, until skin blisters and is slightly blackened. (This may also be done over gas flame holding peppers with a long handled fork.) Place peppers in a paper bag and close bag. When peppers are cool enough to handle, about 5 minutes, trim off tops, remove seeds and peel. Place all ingredients in a blender or a food processor fitted with the metal blade and process to a puree. Makes 4 servings.

Per Serving:
33 Calories, 0mg Chol, 7g Carbo, 1g Prot, 4mg Sodium, 0g Fat (0.1g Sat 0.2g Poly 0g Mono)
Exchanges: 1 vegetable

Sesame Sauce

Serve over meats, chicken, pasta or salad.

Serves: 12 (1-tablespoon) servings
Cooking time: 0
Preparation time: 5 minutes

1 teaspoon grated gingerroot, or 1/2 teaspoon ground ginger
1 teaspoon minced garlic
1/2 cup tomato juice
2 tablespoons sesame oil
2 tablespoons low-sodium soy sauce
1-1/2 teaspoons Dijon-style mustard

Place all ingredients in a jar, close tightly and shake well to combine. Makes about 3/4 cup.

Per Serving:
18 Calories, 0mg Chol, 1g Carbo, 0g Prot, 109mg Sodium, 2g Fat (0.2g Sat 0.2g Poly 0.7g Mono)
Exchanges: free

Tomato Salsa

Serve as a topping for fish, poultry, eggs, pasta or beans.

Serves: 4
Cooking time: 0
Preparation time: 10 minutes .

1-1/4 cups canned Italian plum tomatoes, drained
1/4 cup chopped green onions
1 celery stalk, diced
1 tablespoon fresh lime juice
1 teaspoon minced garlic
2 tablespoons chopped fresh parsley or cilantro
1/4 teaspoon hot red pepper flakes
Pepper to taste

Coarsely chop tomatoes. Combine all ingredients and chill before serving. Makes about 1-1/2 cups.

Per Serving:
20 Calories, 0mg Chol, 5g Carbo, 1g Prot, 130mg Sodium, 0g Fat
Exchanges: 1 vegetable

Breads

One thing that can't be done in short order is baking yeast breads. But there are a number of delicious muffins and quick breads that can be prepared in just a few minutes and baked in less than an hour. These can be baking while you are preparing the rest of the meal. Or you may want to take part of the weekend and bake several batches to store in the freezer for use during the week. Several recipes use already baked French and Italian bread, and we suggest you purchase the freshest and most healthful loaves available, preferably whole grain. Small sizes (6 to 10 ounces) are the best. All of the baked goods presented here are chock-full of healthful ingredients. They contain no sugar, are low in fat and high in fiber.

Blueberry Muffins

Serves: 12
Cooking time: 25 minutes
Preparation time: 15 minutes

1 cup unbleached all-purpose flour
1 cup whole-wheat flour
1 tablespoon baking powder
1/2 teaspoon salt
1-1/2 tablespoons crystalline fructose
1/2 teaspoon ground mace
1 egg
1 cup skim milk
1 teaspoon pure vanilla extract
3 tablespoons walnut oil
1 cup fresh blueberries

Preheat oven to 425F (220C). Coat a 12-cup muffin pan with non-stick cooking spray. Sift dry ingredients into a medium-size bowl. In a small bowl, beat egg lightly and stir in milk, vanilla and walnut oil. Add to dry ingredients and mix until the batter is moist. Fold in blueberries. Spoon into muffin cups and bake 25 minutes until lightly browned. Makes 12 muffins.

Per Serving:
131 Calories, 23mg Chol, 20g Carbo, 4g Prot, 167mg Sodium, 5g Fat (0.7g Sat 2.4g Poly 1.1g Mono)
Exchanges: 1 starch/bread, 1 fat

Cranberry Corn Muffins

Serves: 12
Cooking time: 15 to 20 minutes
Preparation time: 10 minutes

1 cup yellow cornmeal
1/2 cup unbleached all-purpose flour
1/2 cup whole-wheat flour
4 teaspoons baking powder
1 cup skim milk
1 egg, beaten
1/4 cup walnut oil
1 cup fresh cranberries

Preheat oven to 400F (205C). Coat a 12-cup muffin pan with non-stick cooking spray. In a medium-size bowl, combine cornmeal, flours and baking powder. In another bowl, mix milk, egg and oil; stir into the dry ingredients. Fold in cranberries. Spoon batter into muffin cups (2/3 full). Bake 15 to 20 minutes, until golden-brown.

Per Serving:
143 Calories, 23mg Chol, 20g Carbo, 3g Prot, 121mg Sodium, 6g Fat (0.8g Sat 3.1g Poly 1.4g Mono)

Exchanges: 1 starch/bread, 1 fat

Joan's Gourmet Muffins

Serves: 10 (2-muffin) servings
Cooking time: 25 minutes
Preparation time: 10 minutes

1 cup buttermilk
1 egg
1-1/2 tablespoons walnut oil
1 cup unbleached all-purpose flour
1/4 cup whole-wheat flour
1 teaspoon baking powder
1/2 teaspoon baking soda
1/4 teaspoon salt
6 tablespoons grated Parmesan cheese
1/2 teaspoon dried rosemary, crushed

Preheat oven to 350F (175C). Coat 20 mini-muffin cups with non-stick cooking spray. In a small bowl, beat together buttermilk, egg and oil. In a large bowl, sift together flours, baking powder, baking soda and salt. Add 4 tablespoons of the grated cheese and the rosemary; blend. Pour buttermilk mixture into center of flour mixture and mix with a fork until blended but still lumpy. Spoon mixture into muffin cups, filling empty cups with water. Top each muffin with remaining cheese. Place in upper third of oven and bake 20 to 25 minutes, until muffins are golden. Makes 20 mini-muffins.

Per Serving:
56 Calories, 15mg Chol, 7g Carbo, 2g Prot, 103mg Sodium, 2g Fat (0.6g Sat 0.8g Poly 0.6g Mono)
Exchanges: 1/2 starch/bread, 1/2 fat

Raisin Oat Bran Muffins

Serves: 12 (2-muffin) servings
Cooking time: 15 minutes
Preparation time: 10 minutes

1-1/4 cups oat bran
1/4 cup sunflower seeds
2 tablespoons raisins
1 teaspoon baking powder
1 tablespoon crystalline fructose
3/4 cup skim milk
1 egg, beaten
1 tablespoon walnut oil

Preheat oven to 425F (220C). Coat 24 mini-muffin cups with non-stick cooking spray. In a medium-size bowl, combine oat bran, sunflower seeds, raisins, baking powder and fructose. In another bowl, mix together milk, egg and walnut oil; stir into dry ingredients. Spoon batter into muffin cups and bake 15 minutes, until golden. Makes 24 mini-muffins.

Per Serving:
86 Calories, 23mg Chol, 11g Carbo, 3g Prot, 47mg Sodium, 4g Fat (0.6g Sat 1.9g Poly 1.0g Mono)
Exchanges: 1 starch/bread

Parmesan Popovers

Serves: 12
Cooking time: 30 minutes
Preparation time: 10 minutes

4 egg whites, at room temperature
1/2 cup non-fat dry milk powder
1 cup water
3/4 cup unbleached all-purpose flour
1/4 cup whole-wheat flour
2 tablespoons Betty's Butter (page 11)
1/8 teaspoon freshly grated nutmeg
2 tablespoons grated Parmesan cheese

Preheat oven to 450F (230C). Coat a 12-cup muffin pan with non-stick cooking spray. Place all ingredients except the cheese in a blender or a food processor fitted with the metal blade and process 15 to 20 seconds, being careful not to overmix. Pour batter into the muffin cups. Sprinkle each popover with 1/2 teaspoon of grated cheese. Bake 15 minutes; reduce heat to 350F (175C) and bake 15 minutes more. Serve at once. Makes 12 popovers.

Per Serving:
76 Calories, 3mg Chol, 10g Carbo, 4g Prot, 55mg Sodium, 2g Fat (0.8g Sat 0.8g Poly 0.6g Mono)
Exchanges: 1 starch/bread

Buttermilk Blueberry Bake

Serves: 6
Cooking time: 40 minutes
Preparation time: 10 minutes

1/3 cup whole-wheat flour
1/3 cup unbleached all-purpose flour
2 teaspoons baking powder
1 tablespoon crystalline fructose
1 cup buttermilk
2 tablespoons frozen orange juice concentrate
2 cups fresh blueberries
Drained orange yogurt (optional)

Preheat oven to 350F (175C). Coat an 8-inch-square baking pan with non-stick cooking spray. In a medium-size bowl, blend flours, baking powder and fructose. Gradually stir in buttermilk and orange juice and blend. Turn into baking pan and top with berries. Bake until lightly browned, about 40 minutes. Top with a dollop of yogurt, if desired.

Per Serving:
105 Calories, 2mg Chol, 22g Carbo, 3g Prot, 150mg Sodium, 1g Fat (0.3g Sat 0.1g Poly 0.1g Mono)
Exchanges: 1-1/2 starch/bread

Chili-Cheese Corn Bread

Serves: 12
Cooking time: 10 minutes
Preparation time: 10 minutes

1 cup plus 2 tablespoons yellow cornmeal
2 teaspoons baking powder
1/2 teaspoon baking soda
1/2 teaspoon salt
1/4 cup whole-wheat flour
1-1/4 cups buttermilk
1 egg plus 1 egg white, lightly beaten
1/4 cup shredded sharp cheddar cheese
2 tablespoons chopped mild green chile, or to taste

Preheat oven to 450F (230C). Coat an 8-inch-square baking pan with non-stick cooking spray and dust with 2 tablespoons of cornmeal. Sift into a large bowl the remaining cornmeal, baking powder, baking soda, salt and flour. In another bowl, combine buttermilk, eggs, cheese and chile, then stir into the dry ingredients. Pour batter into the prepared baking pan and place in upper third of oven. Bake 10 minutes or until dough is firm in center. Makes 12 (2-inch) pieces.

Per Serving:
98 Calories, 28mg Chol, 15g Carbo, 4g Prot, 253mg Sodium, 2g Fat (1.1g Sat 0.2g Poly 0.6g Mono)
Exchanges: 1 starch/bread, 1/2 fat

Norwegian Nut Bread

Serves: 12
Cooking time: 50 minutes
Preparation time: 15 minutes

1 cup sifted unbleached all-purpose flour
1 teaspoon baking soda
1 teaspoon salt
1/2 cup chopped almonds, filberts and sunflower seeds
1/4 cup non-fat dry milk powder
1 cup unsifted whole-wheat flour
1/2 cup raisins
1 tablespoon grated orange zest
1 egg, beaten
1 cup buttermilk
2 tablespoons walnut oil

Preheat oven to 375F (190C). Coat 2 empty 16-ounce cans with non-stick cooking spray. In a medium-size bowl, combine flour, baking soda, salt, nuts, dry milk, whole-wheat flour, raisins and orange zest. In a small bowl, combine egg, buttermilk and walnut oil; add to flour mixture and blend well. Spoon batter into cans and bake 50 minutes or until golden. Loosen bread from cans with a small spatula and cool on rack. Makes 2 small loaves, about 6 slices each.

Per Serving:
151 Calories, 24mg Chol, 23g Carbo, 5g Prot, 254mg Sodium, 5g Fat (0.8g Sat 2.0g Poly 1.8g Mono)
Exchanges: 1-1/2 starch/bread, 1/2 fat

Scottish Scones

Serves: 16
Cooking time: 15 to 20 minutes
Preparation time: 15 minutes

1 cup unbleached all-purpose flour
1 cup whole-wheat flour
1 teaspoon baking powder
1/2 teaspoon salt
4 tablespoons whipped butter
1 cup buttermilk
1/2 cup golden raisins

Preheat oven to 400F (205C). Coat a baking sheet with non-stick cooking spray. In a medium-size bowl, sift dry ingredients together. Add butter, mixing into flour with your fingers. Add buttermilk and knead to a soft (sticky) dough. Knead in raisins. On a floured board, roll out dough to 1/2 inch thick. Cut in 16 rounds. Place on a baking sheet and bake 15 to 20 minutes, until golden. Makes 16 scones.

Per Serving:
97 Calories, 7mg Chol, 16g Carbo, 3g Prot, 115mg Sodium, 3g Fat (1.5g Sat 0.2g Poly 0.7g Mono)
Exchanges: 1 starch/bread

Garlic Bread

Serves: 10
Cooking time: 20 minutes
Preparation time: 10 minutes

1 (10-oz.) loaf Italian bread
4 garlic cloves, minced
1/4 cup virgin olive oil
1/4 cup chopped fresh parsley

Preheat oven to 350F (175C). Slice bread in half lengthwise. Mix together garlic, olive oil and parsley in a small bowl. Spread on cut sides of bread. Place on a baking sheet. Bake 20 minutes or until crisp. Slice and serve.

Per Serving:
131 Calories, 0mg Chol, 16g Carbo, 3g Prot, 152mg Sodium, 6g Fat (1.0g Sat 0.5g Poly 4.5g Mono)
Exchanges: 1 starch/bread, 1 fat

Sesame Bread

Serves: 12
Cooking time: 20 minutes
Preparation time: 10 minutes

1 (12-oz.) loaf French bread
1/4 cup virgin olive oil
1/4 cup chopped fresh parsley
1/4 cup chopped chives
2 tablespoons sesame seeds

Preheat oven to 350F (175C). Slice bread lengthwise. Combine oil, parsley and chives in a small bowl; spread on cut side of bread. Sprinkle with sesame seeds. Place on a baking sheet. Bake 20 minutes or until bread is crisp.

Per Serving:
131 Calories, 0mg Chol, 16g Carbo, 3g Prot, 154mg Sodium, 5g Fat (1.0g Sat 0.7g Poly 4.1g Mono)

Exchanges: 1 starch/bread, 1 fat

Desserts

Now we come to our just desserts. Many cookbooks written for those with diabetes offer versions of chocolate cake and other baked goodies loaded with sugar or sugar substitutes. When it comes to dessert, my personal choice is any one of many delicious combinations of fruit, yogurt or whipped cottage or ricotta cheese. I prefer a simple fruit for dessert. There are some pie crusts in the Basics chapter which may be filled with fruit combinations or cheese mixtures. Most of these dessert offerings are healthful, refreshing and provide a light and fitting end to all the good dishes preceding. Eat, enjoy and be healthy!

Apricot Mousse

This mousse can also be spooned into a baked pie crust before chilling.

Serves: 4
Cooking time: 0
Preparation time: 10 minutes + 30 minutes soaking time

1 cup dried apricots or prunes
1 cup soft tofu (bean curd)
2 teaspoons pure vanilla extract
2 tablespoons non-fat dry milk powder
2 egg whites, at room temperature
Fresh mint

Soak apricots in hot water 30 minutes; drain, reserving water. In a blender or a food processor fitted with the metal blade, place tofu, apricots, vanilla and dry milk and process. Add some of the apricot water, if necessary, to process. Whip egg whites until stiff but not dry. Place apricot mixture in a medium-size bowl and fold in egg whites. Spoon into dessert glasses, garnish with mint and serve chilled. Makes about 3-1/2 cups.

Per Serving:
84 Calories, 0mg Chol, 12g Carbo, 6g Prot, 42mg Sodium, 2g Fat (0.3g Sat 1.0g Poly 0.4g Mono)

Exchanges: 1 fruit, 1/2 meat (if egg whites are used)

Variation: This may also be made with a combination of prunes and apricots. The egg whites may be omitted for a pudding-like consistency. Without egg whites, this makes 2-1/2 cups.

Banana-Berry-Rice Pudding

Serves: 6
Cooking time: 20 minutes for rice, 1 hour baking
Preparation time: 25 minutes

1 cup cooked brown rice
1/2 cup mashed banana
1/2 cup nonfat-dry milk powder
3/4 cup water
1 teaspoon maple extract
1 teaspoon ground cinnamon
1 teaspoon toasted sesame seeds
1/4 cup frozen orange juice concentrate
2 tablespoons fresh blueberries, or 1 tablespoon raisins
2 egg whites, beaten stiff
1 tablespoon sunflower seeds

Preheat oven to 350F (175C). Mix together all ingredients except egg whites and sunflower seeds. Fold egg whites into rice mixture and pour into 4-inch by 8-inch baking pan. Top with sprinkling of sunflower seeds. Bake for 1 hour or until pudding is set.

Per Serving:
114 Calories, 1mg Chol, 21g Carbo, 5g Prot, 53mg Sodium, 1.4g Fat (0.2g Sat 0.7g Poly 0.4g Mono)

Exchanges: 1 starch/bread, 1/2 fruit

Banana-Sweet Potato Pudding

Serves: 6
Cooking time: 35 minutes
Preparation time: 25 minutes

**1/2 pound sweet potatoes, peeled and cubed
(about 1 cup)**
1/4 cup water
2 medium bananas, sliced
**1 cup non-fat milk mixed with 2 tablespoons non-fat dry
milk powder**
1/2 teaspoon coconut extract
1 small cinnamon stick
1 tablespoon frozen orange juice concentrate
1/2 teaspoon pure vanilla extract
2 tablespoons slivered almonds

Boil the sweet potatoes in water for 20 minutes or until
tender. Drain off any excess water and add bananas,
milk, coconut extract, cinnamon stick and orange juice
concentrate. Cook about 15 minutes or until thick.
Remove cinnamon stick and add vanilla. Puree in
blender or food processor and serve either warm or
chilled, topped with slivered almonds.

Per Serving:
102 Calories, 1mg Chol, 19g Carbo, 3g Prot, 32mg Sodium,
1.8g Fat (0.3g Sat, 0.4g Poly, 0.9g Mono)

Exchanges: 1 starch/bread, 1/2 fat

Banana Tofu Cream

Serves: 4
Cooking time: 0
Preparation time: 5 minutes

2 medium-size bananas, frozen
3/4 cup soft tofu (bean curd)
4 ice cubes, crushed
1 teaspoon crystalline fructose
1 teaspoon molasses
1/4 teaspoon freshly grated nutmeg
1/4 cup non-fat dry milk powder
1/2 cup water
1/2 teaspoon pure vanilla extract
1 tablespoon chopped walnuts

Slice bananas. In a blender or a food processor fitted with the metal blade, place bananas and remaining ingredients except walnuts. Process until smooth. Spoon into a bowl and freeze to a pudding-like consistency before serving. Do not freeze hard. Garnish with chopped walnuts.

Per Serving:
126 Calories, 2mg Chol, 21g Carbo, 6g Prot, 56mg Sodium, 3g Fat
(0.5g Sat 1.5g Poly 0.6g Mono)
Exchanges: 1 fruit, 1/2 milk

Baked Apples Burnette

Serves: 4
Cooking time: 30 to 35 minutes
Preparation time: 10 minutes

4 MacIntosh or Rome apples
2 tablespoons raisins
1 tablespoon sunflower seeds
1/2 teaspoon ground cinnamon
1/4 teaspoon freshly grated nutmeg
Few drops pure vanilla extract
1/4 cup water
1 tablespoon frozen orange juice concentrate

Preheat oven to 375F (190C). Core apples and peel away about 1/2 inch of skin from top of each. Prick each a few times with a fork. Fill each core with raisins, sunflower seeds, cinnamon, nutmeg and a drop of vanilla. Place apples in a baking dish and add water mixed with orange juice. Bake 30 to 35 minutes until apples are soft, basting occasionally with liquid. Serve warm or chilled with syrup.

Per Serving:
96 Calories, 0mg Chol, 22g Carbo, 1g Prot, 2mg Sodium, 1g Fat (0.2g Sat 0.8g Poly 0.2g Mono)
Exchanges: 1-1/2 fruit

Berry Bonanza

Serves: 4
Cooking time: 0
Preparation time: 15 minutes

1 cup fresh blueberries
1 cup sliced fresh strawberries
1 cup cubed cantaloupe or other melon
2 tablespoons frozen orange juice concentrate
1 tablespoon fresh lime juice
1/4 teaspoon ground cinnamon
1 teaspoon grated orange zest

Layer fruit in a serving bowl. Mix orange juice, lime juice and cinnamon; spoon over fruit. Top with orange zest.

Per Serving:
62 Calories, 0mg Chol, 15g Carbo, 1g Prot, 6mg Sodium, 0g Fat
Exchanges: 1 fruit

Bubbly Blueberries

Serves: 4
Cooking time: 0
Preparation time: 5 minutes

3 cups fresh blueberries
1/4 cup orange juice
1/4 cup diet ginger ale

Put blueberries in a serving bowl. Combine orange juice and ginger ale and pour over berries.

Per Serving:
71 Calories, 0mg Chol, 18g Carbo, 1g Prot, 8mg Sodium, 0g Fat

Exchanges: 1 fruit

Variation: Strawberries, raspberries, blackberries, melon or other fruit may be substituted for blueberries.

Coffee Cream Pudding

Serves: 4
Cooking time: 0
Preparation time: 25 minutes

1 envelope unflavored gelatin
1/4 cup frozen orange juice concentrate
1 cup strong freshly brewed coffee
1 tablespoon crystalline fructose
1 cup low-fat cottage cheese
1/4 cup part-skim ricotta cheese
1 egg, separated
4 tablespoons sugar-free fruit conserve (raspberry, peach
   or any flavor desired)
12 almonds and filberts

In a small bowl, sprinkle the gelatin on the concentrated orange juice. Add coffee and fructose. Stir to dissolve gelatin. Place cottage cheese and ricotta in food processor container, drop in egg yolk and process. Add gelatin mixture and repeat. Pour into metal tray and place in freezer for no more than 30 minutes, so that it does not freeze. In the meantime, whip the egg white until it is stiff. Remove cottage cheese mixture from freezer and fold in egg white. Turn into individual molds or 1, 3-cup ring mold. Into the center of each portion place 1/2 tablespoon of the fruit conserve. Refrigerate until set. When ready to serve, unmold by dipping in hot water for a second or loosening with a sharp knife. Top with remaining fruit conserve and some nuts. May also be served with orange slices or other fresh fruit.

Per Serving:
192 Calories, 63mg Chol, 23g Carbo, 13g Prot, 274mg Sodium, 4.6g Fat (1.9g Sat 0.5g Poly 1.8g Mono)

Exchanges: 1 1/2 fruit, 1 1/2 meat

Coffee Custard Cups

Serves: 4
Cooking time: 45 minutes
Preparation time: 15 minutes

2 eggs (1 yolk only)
1 cup evaporated non-fat milk
1 teaspoon instant coffee granules
1/2 teaspoon pure vanilla extract
1 tablespoon frozen orange juice concentrate
1 tablespoon grated orange zest
Ground cinnamon

Preheat oven to 350F (175C). Process eggs in blender, then add evaporated milk, instant coffee, vanilla and orange juice concentrate. Pour into 4 individual custard cups and place in large baking pan filled with about 1 inch of boiling water. Bake for 45 minutes or until a knife inserted in the center comes out clean. Remove from oven, chill, run a knife around edges of cups, invert and garnish each custard with sprinkling of orange zest and cinnamon.

Per Serving:
84 Calories, 55mg Chol, 10g Carbo, 7g Prot, 103mg Sodium, 1.4g Fat (0.5g Sat 0.2g Poly 0.5g Mono)

Exchanges: 1/2 milk, 1/2 meat

Creamy Cantaloupe

Serves: 4
Cooking time: 0
Preparation time: 15 minutes

2 cups cubed cantaloupe
1/2 cup plain low-fat yogurt
2 tablespoons part-skim ricotta cheese
1 tablespoon frozen grape juice concentrate
Ground cinnamon
1 tablespoon slivered almonds

Place cantaloupe in a serving bowl. Blend yogurt and ricotta; stir in grape juice. Spoon over the melon and top with a sprinkling of cinnamon and slivered almonds.

Per Serving:
64 Calories, 3mg Chol, 11g Carbo, 3g Prot, 37mg Sodium, 2g Fat (0.4g Sat 0.2g Poly 0.6g Mono)
Exchanges: 1 fruit

Fresh Fruit Medley

Serves: 4
Cooking time: 0
Preparation time: 15 minutes

1 small apple, peeled and diced
1/2 medium-size banana, sliced
1 small orange, sectioned
1/2 cup seedless grapes
1 tablespoon frozen orange juice concentrate
1/4 cup plain low-fat yogurt
2 tablespoons part-skim ricotta cheese
1/8 teaspoon ground ginger
1/8 teaspoon ground cinnamon
1/2 teaspoon pure vanilla extract
4 walnut halves

Place all fruit in a bowl and mix in frozen orange juice concentrate. In a blender, combine yogurt, ricotta, ginger, cinnamon and vanilla. Portion the fruit into dessert bowls, top each with yogurt-ricotta sauce and garnish with a walnut half.

Other fruits may be substituted, such as melon, kiwifruit, strawberries, blueberries, pears or pineapple. The fruit medley may also be served without the topping.

Per Serving:
87 Calories, 2mg Chol, 17g Carbo, 2g Prot, 20mg Sodium, 2g Fat (0.5g Sat 0.9g Poly 0.5g Mono)
Exchanges: 1 fruit, 1/2 fat

Fudge Freeze

Serves: 4
Cooking time: 2 minutes
Preparation time: 10 minutes

1 cup non-fat milk
3 eggs (1 yolk only)
1 teaspoon pure vanilla extract
1/4 cup carob powder
2 tablespoons non-fat dry milk powder
1 teaspoon instant coffee granules
2 teaspoons crystalline fructose
Dash salt
1 tablespoon roughly chopped hazelnuts

Heat the milk in a small saucepan to scald and remove from heat. Place remaining ingredients except hazelnuts in a blender. Cover and process on slow, then remove cover and pour in hot milk. Process again for about a minute. Turn into metal tray and place in freezer, stirring periodically to break up ice crystals. Stir in hazelnuts before serving.

Per Serving:
95 Calories, 70mg Chol, 13g Carbo, 7g Prot, 89mg Sodium, 2.5g Fat (0.6g Sat 0.4g Poly 1.5g Mono)

Exchanges: 1 starch/bread, 1/2 fat

Iced Mocha Sherbet

Serves: 4
Cooking time: 0
Preparation time: 15 minutes + freeze time

1 1/2 cups evaporated non-fat milk
1 teaspoon pure vanilla extract
2 tablespoons carob powder
1 tablespoon crystalline fructose
2 tablespoons frozen orange juice concentrate
1 tablespoon instant coffee granules
1 tablespoon part-skim ricotta cheese

Mix all ingredients together in blender and turn into metal trays. Place in freezer and stir with fork from time to time to break up ice crystals. When ready to serve, process again so the sherbet is soft.

Per Serving:
121 Calories, 5mg Chol, 22g Carbo, 8g Prot, 117mg Sodium, 0.5g Fat (0.3g Sat 0g Poly 0.2g Mono)

Exchanges: 1 milk, 1/2 fruit

Kiwifruit & Strawberries

Raspberries, blueberries or blackberries may be substituted for strawberries.

Serves: 4
Cooking time: 0
Preparation time: 15 minutes

2 kiwifruit
2 cups fresh strawberries
1 tablespoon frozen orange juice concentrate mixed with 1 tablespoon water
1 teaspoon toasted pine nuts

Peel kiwifruit and slice in thin rounds. Arrange on dessert plates. Wash, hull and slice the strawberries and arrange them over the kiwifruit. Drizzle orange juice over each dish and top with pine nuts.

Per Serving:
54 Calories, 0mg Chol, 12g Carbo, 1g Prot, 3mg Sodium, 1g Fat (0.1g Sat 0.3g Poly 0.2g Mono)
Exchanges: 1 fruit

Mocha Mousse

Spoon over fruit, ladyfingers, graham crackers, or pour into a baked pie crust.

Serves: 6
Cooking time: 0
Preparation time: 5 minutes

1 cup part-skim ricotta cheese
1/4 cup low-fat (1%) cottage cheese
1 teaspoon ground cinnamon
2 teaspoons powdered instant coffee
1/2 teaspoon pure vanilla extract
1 tablespoon frozen orange juice concentrate
2 tablespoons blanched slivered almonds
Fruit, ladyfingers, graham crackers or baked pie crust (optional)

Blend all ingredients except almonds in a blender or a food processor fitted with the metal blade. Top with almonds.

Per Serving:
72 Calories, 11mg Chol, 4g Carbo, 5g Prot, 76mg Sodium, 4g Fat (1.9g Sat 0.3g Poly 1.4g Mono)
Exchanges: 1/2 milk, 1 fat

Papaya with Blueberry Sauce

Cantaloupe, mango, or peaches may be substituted for papaya.

Serves: 4
Cooking time: 10 minutes
Preparation time: 10 minutes

1 ripe papaya
1 cup fresh blueberries
2 tablespoons frozen orange juice concentrate
1 teaspoon grated orange zest
Ground cinnamon
4 teaspoons plain low-fat yogurt
1/2 teaspoon pure vanilla extract

Peel and seed papaya; slice into 12 thin wedges. Arrange on four dessert plates and refrigerate. Meanwhile, in a small saucepan, cook blueberries with orange juice, orange zest and cinnamon, stirring, until berries are soft and cooked down to a sauce, about 10 minutes. Pour into a small bowl, cover and refrigerate until chilled. Mix yogurt with vanilla. When ready to serve, spoon blueberry sauce over papaya and top with dollop of vanilla yogurt. Sauce cooks down to about 2/3 cup.

Per Serving:
68 Calories, 0mg Chol, 17g Carbo, 1g Prot, 8mg Sodium, 0g Fat
Exchanges: 1 fruit

Peach Freeze

Serves: 4
Cooking time: 0
Preparation time: 15 minutes

2 cups peeled, pitted and mashed fresh peaches
1 cup plain non-fat yogurt
1 teaspoon pure vanilla extract
2 tablespoons unflavored gelatin
2 tablespoons frozen orange juice concentrate
1 tablespoon grated orange zest
Toasted sesame seeds
Ground cinnamon

Combine peaches, yogurt and vanilla until well mixed.
Sprinkle the gelatin over the orange juice concentrate
and wait 5 minutes before dissolving the gel over hot
water. Then combine with peach mixture. Place in metal
tray, cover and put in freezer for about 1 hour, stirring
periodically. Do not allow this to freeze solid. Before
serving, stir again, spoon into 4 dessert glasses and top
with grated orange zest, sesame seeds and cinnamon.

Per Serving:
138 Calories, 1mg Chol, 28g Carbo, 8g Prot, 54mg Sodium,
0.3g Fat (0.1g Sat 0.1g Poly 0.1g Mono)

Exchanges: 2 fruit

Peach Melba

Serves: 4
Cooking time: 2 minutes
Preparation time: 15 minutes

4 large ripe peaches
1 cup plus 2 tablespoons raspberries
1/2 cup part-skim ricotta cheese
**2 tablespoons non-fat dry milk powder plus water to
    make 1/4 cup**
1 tablespoon unsweetened grape juice

Blanch peaches by dropping them In boiling water for
30 seconds. Remove, run under cold water and peel off
skins. Cut in half, discard pits and place 2 peach halves
on each of 4 individual dessert dishes. Puree raspberries with remaining ingredients, reserving 2 tablespoons
of berries for garnish. Spoon puree over peaches, top
with berries and serve cold.

Per Serving:
112 Calories, 10mg Chol, 18g Carbo, 5g Prot, 50mg Sodium,
2.7g Fat (1.5g Sat 0.2g Poly 0.8g Mono)

Exchanges: 1 fruit, 1 meat

Peach Poach

Serves: 4
Cooking time: 15 minutes
Preparation time: 10 minutes

1/2 cup water
1 teaspoon crystalline fructose
1 cinnamon stick
4 peaches, peeled, halved
1/2 banana

In a medium-size saucepan, bring water, fructose and cinnamon stick to a boil. Reduce heat, add peach halves, cover and cook 10 minutes. Place in a small bowl and refrigerate until chilled. Discard cinnamon stick, slice banana and add to peaches.

Per Serving:
64 Calories, 0mg Chol, 16g Carbo, 1g Prot, 0mg Sodium, 0g Fat
Exchanges: 1 fruit

Peanut Custard

Serves: 4
Cooking time: 45 minutes
Preparation time: 15 minutes

2 tablespoons peanut butter
1 cup evaporated non-fat milk, divided
2 eggs (1 yolk only)
1/2 teaspoon pure vanilla extract
4 teaspoons chopped roasted peanuts

Preheat oven to 350F (175C). Stir together the peanut butter and 1/2 cup of the milk in small bowl. In a separate bowl, whisk the eggs and add the remaining milk, then the peanut butter mixture and vanilla. Turn into a small ovenproof baking dish or into 4 individual custard cups and place in a large pan containing about 1 inch of boiling water. Bake for about 45 minutes or until a knife inserted in the center comes out clean. Cool, turn out onto dessert dishes, and serve garnished with peanuts.

Per Serving:
139 Calories, 55mg Chol, 10g Carbo, 10g Prot, 140mg Sodium, 7.0g Fat (1.5g Sat 1.8g Poly 3.2g Mono)

Exchanges: 1/2 milk, 1 meat, 1 fat

Pear & Apple Sauce

Serves: 4
Cooking time: 10 to 20 minutes
Preparation time: 10 minutes

2 ripe Anjou or Bose pears
2 Granny Smith or Golden Delicious apples
1/2 cup fresh cranberries
2 tablespoons frozen orange juice concentrate
1 cinnamon stick
1/2 teaspoon pure vanilla extract
1/4 teaspoon freshly grated nutmeg
4 walnut halves

Cut pears and apples in half and core. Place in a medium-size saucepan with remaining ingredients except walnuts and bring to a boil. Reduce heat, cover and simmer over low heat 10 to 20 minutes until fruit is tender. Discard cinnamon stick. Strain through food mill and serve warm or chilled, topped with a walnut half.

Per Serving:
95 Calories, 0mg Chol, 21g Carbo, 1g Prot, 1mg Sodium, 2g Fat (0.2g Sat 0.9g Poly 0.3g Mono)
Exchanges: 1-1/2 fruit

Poached Pears

Serves: 4
Cooking time: 20 minutes
Preparation time: 10 minutes

4 small ripe Anjou or Bosc pears
1/2 cup unsweetened apple juice
1 tablespoon fresh lime juice
1 cinnamon stick
2 whole cloves
2 tablespoons slivered almonds

Preheat oven to 350F (175C). Peel pears, core and cut in half. Place in a glass baking dish. Combine remaining ingredients and pour over pears. Cover with foil and bake 20 minutes. Discard cinnamon stick and serve warm or cool, with a garnish of slivered almonds.

Per Serving:
80 Calories, 0mg Chol, 17g Carbo, 1g Prot, 1mg Sodium, 2g Fat (0.2g Sat 0.4g Poly 1.0g Mono)
Exchanges: 1 fruit

Raspberry Parfait

Serves: 4
Cooking time: 0
Preparation time: 20 minutes

1 envelope unflavored gelatin
1/4 cup cold water
10 ounces frozen unsweetened raspberries, thawed
1 cup plain non-fat yogurt
1/2 teaspoon pure vanilla extract
2 egg whites at room temperature
1 teaspoon crystalline fructose
1 tablespoon slivered blanched almonds

In a mixing bowl, soften the gelatin in cold water and then place over hot water to dissolve. Stir in the raspberries, yogurt, and vanilla and chill. In the meantime, beat egg whites until frothy and add the fructose. Beat again until peaks form, then fold into the raspberry mixture. Chill until set. Serve in parfait glasses, topped with slivered almonds.

Per Serving:
96 Calories, 1mg Chol, 13g Carbo, 7g Prot, 78mg Sodium, 1.2g Fat (0.1g Sat 0.3g Poly 0.7g Mono)

Exchanges: 1 fruit, 1/2 fat

Strawberry Frost

This is good with raspberries or blackberries as well. It may be placed in a bowl, covered and frozen up to 1-1/2 hours.

Serves: 4
Cooking time: 0
Preparation time: 10 minutes

1-1/4 cups plain low-fat yogurt
1/4 cup part-skim ricotta cheese
2 cups frozen strawberries (no sugar added)
1 teaspoon pure vanilla extract
1 tablespoon frozen orange juice concentrate
Extra strawberries for garnish
Few sprigs fresh mint (optional)

In a blender or a food processor fitted with a metal blade, place yogurt, ricotta, strawberries, vanilla and orange juice; process until smooth. Spoon into parfait glasses and garnish with berries and a mint sprig, if desired. Serve at once.

Per Serving:
81 Calories, 6mg Chol, 13g Carbo, 5g Prot, 72mg Sodium, 1g Fat (0.8g Sat 0.1g Poly 0.3g Mono)
Exchanges: 1/2 milk, 1/2 fruit

Vienna Cream

Serve over
ladyfingers,
graham crackers
and fresh fruit, or
pour into a baked
pie crust.

Serves: 4 to 6
Cooking time: 0
Preparation time: 10 minutes

3/4 cup plain low-fat yogurt
1/2 cup part-skim ricotta cheese
2 tablespoons molasses
4 tablespoons chopped almonds and filberts
3 tablespoons chopped dried figs or raisins

Blend yogurt, ricotta cheese and molasses until smooth. Stir in remaining ingredients. Chill to blend flavors. Makes 2 cups.

Per Serving:
125 Calories, 9g Chol, 15g Carbo, 6g Prot, 70mg Sodium, 5g Fat
(1.6g Sat 0.7g Poly 2.4g Mono)
Exchanges: 1 milk, 1 fat

Delicious Dessert Dressing

Serve as a topping for baked goods or fruit.

Serves: 12 (1-tablespoon) servings
Cooking time: 0
Preparation time: 5 minutes

1 small banana
1/2 cup non-fat yogurt
1 teaspoon frozen orange juice concentrate
1 teaspoon poppy seeds

Place all ingredients except poppy seeds in a blender or a food processor fitted with the metal blade and process to a puree. Stir in poppy seeds. Makes 3/4 cup.

Per Serving:
15 Calories, 0mg Chol, 3g Carbo, 1g Prot, 8mg Sodium, 0g Fat
Exchanges: free

Index

C